MAKERS
of the
MUSLIM
WORLD

Ahmad ibn Tulun

TITLES IN THE MAKERS OF THE MUSLIM WORLD SERIES

Series Editors: Professor Khaled El-Rouayheb, Harvard University, and
Professor Sabine Schmidtke, Institute for Advanced Study, Princeton

For current information and details of other books in the series, please visit
oneworld-publications.com/makers-of-the-muslim-world

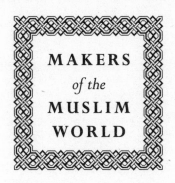

MAKERS
of the
MUSLIM
WORLD

Ahmad ibn Tulun

Governor of Abbasid Egypt,

868–884

MATTHEW S. GORDON

ONEWORLD
ACADEMIC

Oneworld Academic

An imprint of Oneworld Publications

Published by Oneworld Academic in 2021

ISBN 978-1-85168-809-8
eISBN 978-1-78607-994-7

Maps © Erica Milwain

Ibn Tulun mosque photograph © Nader El Assy/Shutterstock;
Tulunid gold dinar photographs courtesy of the
American Numismatic Society.

Typeset by Geethik Technologies
Printed and bound in Great Britain by Clays Ltd, Elcograf S.p.A.

Oneworld Publications
10 Bloomsbury Street
London WC1B 3SR
England

Stay up to date with the latest books,
special offers, and exclusive content from
Oneworld with our newsletter

Sign up on our website
oneworld-publications.com

To S., beloved

Men cheered, applauded his prowess. All this quite formal, and not to be taken literally. He would pour a libation, and with the gods' assent some of the boar's fierce energy, and hot muscle and hotter breath, would fatten his spirit. It was a mystery. Part of a world of ceremony, of high play, that was eternal and had nothing to do with the actual and immediate, with *this* particular occasion, or *this* boar, or *this* king. Even the landscape it took place in was freed of its particular elements…all this was to be ignored, left to fall away into the confused and confusing realm of the incidental and ordinary.

David Malouf, Ransom

It was not hard to imagine why this square had been chosen for the niche where the severed heads of rebel viziers or ill-starred senior officials were placed. Perhaps nowhere else could the eyes of passers-by so easily grasp the interdependency between the imposing solidity of the ancient square and the human heads that had dared to show it disrespect. It was clear at once that the niche had been sited in the wall to convey the impression that the head's lifeless eyes surveilled every corner of the square. In this way, even the feeblest and least imaginative passer-by could visualize, at least for the moment, his own head displayed at this unnatural height.

Ismail Kadare, The Traitor's Niche

CONTENTS

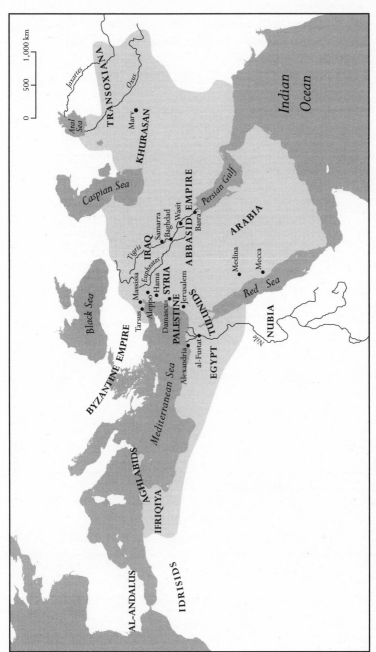

The Abbasid Empire c. 750–900 CE

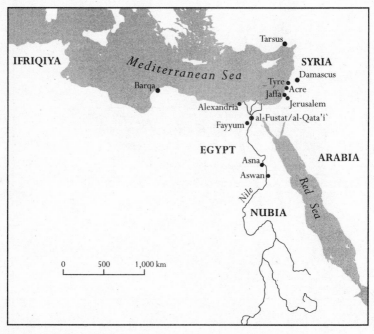

Egypt and Syria c. ninth century CE

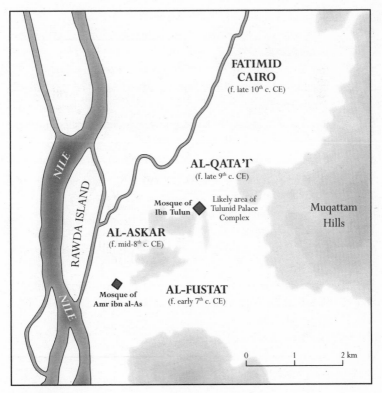

FATIMID
CAIRO
(f. late 10th c. CE)

AL-QATA'I'
(f. late 9th c. CE)

Mosque of
Ibn Tulun

Likely area of
Tulunid Palace
Complex

Muqattam
Hills

AL-ASKAR
(f. mid-8th c. CE)

NILE

RAWDA ISLAND

NILE

Mosque of
Amr ibn al-As

AL-FUSTAT
(f. early 7th c. CE)

0   1   2 km

Al-Qata'i'

CHRONOLOGY

835   Birth of Ahmad ibn Tulun (Baghdad).

838   Abbasid court and army settled in Samarra.

864   Birth of Abu al-Jaysh Khumarawayh.

865   Civil war in Iraq; al-Musta'in dethroned; Ibn Tulun assigned as his guard.

868   Ibn Tulun, appointed resident governor, enters Egypt.

869   Yarjukh confirms Ibn Tulun in office; onset of Zanj war in southern Iraq.

870   Ibn Tulun's aborted campaign into Syria; work commences on al-Qata'i'; al-Mu'tamid assumes the caliphate (870–892).

873   Ibn Tulun assumes control of Egypt's fiscal administration.

877   Deaths of Musa ibn Bugha and Amajur; Ibn Tulun's second campaign into Syria.

879   Mosque of Ibn Tulun completed.

881   Al-Abbas escorted in chains back to Egypt.

882   Lu'lu' defects to al-Muwaffaq; Ibn Tulun's third campaign into Syria.

883   Damascus Assembly; Ibn Tulun, on the frontier, falls ill.

884   Death of Ibn Tulun; succession of Khumarawayh; likely murder of al-Abbas.

891   Death of al-Muwaffaq.

905   Al-Qata'i' falls to Abbasid forces under Muhammad ibn Sulayman.

THE TULUNID HOUSEHOLD

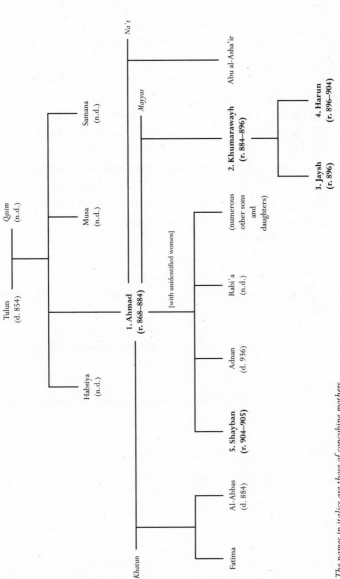

The names in italics are those of concubine mothers.

The names in bold are those of the ruling members of the Tulunid dynasty.

INTRODUCTION

Travelers to modern-day Cairo know Ahmad ibn Tulun from the elegant mosque that bears his name. A centerpiece of the city's extraordinary architectural legacy, it is the oldest of Egypt's original mosques. Its features include graceful arcaded halls, an expansive courtyard, and a harmony of its many parts. The mosque underwent renovations later in the medieval period, notably under Husam al-Din Lajin (r. 1296–1299), a thirteenth-century Egyptian strongman. These included the addition of a domed ablution fountain; additions to the original *mihrab* (the prayer niche, which identifies the proper direction of prayer); and the spiral-shaped minaret (the tower from which, typically, Muslims are summoned to prayer) that stands today. But the principal structure remains as constructed under Ibn Tulun's careful eye. Its survival is remarkable given Cairo's long history of earthquakes and its seismic political past. Refurbished again in the twentieth century, the mosque functions today as a *masjid* (local Muslim prayer hall) and significant tourist site.

The building, for most of its history, has been enveloped by Cairo, a dynamic, crowded metropolis, in the later medieval period as it is today. But Cairo was founded in the late tenth century, well after Ibn Tulun's sojourn in office. The governor (Ar., *amir*) and his ninth-century contemporaries viewed the mosque in a more modest setting. Its size, then, must have left an impression: built on a monumental plan, it loomed over the commercial and residential neighborhoods that surrounded it.

There was, however, a good deal more to the structure than its bulk. Ibn Tulun intended the mosque to signal his abiding commitment to Islam and the duties of his fellow Muslims. Much will be said later of his adherence to the faith. The building was likewise a political gesture: Ibn Tulun built it early in his tenure precisely at the point of consolidating his hold over Egypt. The mosque thus joined piety to power, and the *amir* knew to associate himself with the potent mix.

And there was the building's cost: Ibn Tulun's biographers make much of the sums spent on the project. The quality of workmanship – delicate plaster carving, fine woodwork, and a variety of innovative architectural details – remains in evidence today. This was the work of skilled and, one thinks, well-paid artisans. Such costs cannot have been lost on Ibn Tulun's contemporaries. One source, in fact, describes angry accusations leveled at the governor that the moneys in question must have come from corrupt sources. The mosque, then, spoke of the wealth to which its patron had access and his efforts at directing it to secure his considerable political aims.

Ibn Tulun governed Egypt for sixteen years (868–884). He did so on behalf of the Abbasid dynasty, at that point over a century in power. In this sense among others, he was the product of empire. Baghdad born, he was raised in Samarra, a sprawling city located north on the Tigris River and founded, in the 830s, to replace Baghdad as the empire's hub. Like his father before him, Ibn Tulun served in the imperial military, in Iraq and on the Abbasid-Byzantine frontier in

A view of Ibn Tulun's mosque. The domed structure and circular minaret are likely later replacements of two original Tulunid-era structures. The image captures, however, the expanse and elegance of the original building.

northern Syria. It was as an imperial appointee – his official position was resident governor – that he departed Samarra, at age thirty-four, to take up duties in Egypt. Throughout he retained close ties to the imperial center and, in his fashion, devoted much effort to defending the Abbasid polity.

But had Ibn Tulun been little more than a dutiful imperial servant, there would be little point to this book. It is the pursuit on his part of an ambitious political agenda that draws our interest. To his opponents, and there were many, the *amir* became a renegade, a threat to Abbasid sovereignty and the integrity of the empire. The accusations mounted, and Ibn Tulun devoted much effort in fending off each such charge. There is much to learn of his aims, of course, in these responses. On two points, it seems we can take him on his word: Ibn Tulun never pursued either fully independent rule over Egypt or the demise of the Abbasid regime. Nearly all the written and physical evidence supports this view. Again, he remained committed to the Abbasid caliphate, in title and practice alike, for the duration of his time in office.

But, in the pursuit of his goals, he did confront his imperial masters, and thus roiled political waters. Contemporary and later observers took notice. In his *Sirat Ahmad ibn Tulun*, a biography of the governor, Abdallah ibn Muhammad al-Balawi (fl. late tenth century) describes the younger Ibn Tulun as "forceful, headstrong," a view shared by nearly every other surviving source. The *amir*, as these many references suggest, brought a new aggressive style both to his administration of Egypt and interactions with the imperial state. Small wonder that his relations with the Abbasid house grew strained. Indeed, on at least one occasion, the Abbasids attempted to remove him by force.

What follows is a political biography, an account of one medieval Near Eastern power broker's approach to office. It turns, in good part, on the problem of understanding these seeming contradictions of Ibn Tulun's tenure as governor, then as ruler of Egypt. My argument is that Ibn Tulun sought a delicate balance: a commitment to the survival of the Abbasid house, on the one hand, and a willingness to shake the prevailing political order, on the other. Was he successful? The indications are that he overstepped his limits, a wrinkle to be explored further on.

The drama of Ibn Tulun's career is of interest in its own right. To effect his aims, the *amir* donned a number of hats. He became the *paterfamilias* of an unwieldy and highly visible household. A devout Muslim, he turned routinely to demonstrations of piety, right-mindedness, and charity. Frequently a severe decision maker, he confronted his opponents, when needed, with cruelty and violence, but knew also to extend mercy and even kindness. And, a successful dynast, he founded a regional state. Each facet of the man speaks to his reputation in Islamic and Near Eastern history. Each is a topic deserving of close study. But no less interesting is what his tenure tells us of the politics of the early medieval Islamic period. Tracing the *amir*'s career allows us to take the measure of the Abbasid Empire from a significant provincial perspective. At one time a pre-eminent world power, the later ninth-century Abbasid state was much reduced, a once-great imperial polity struggling not simply for relevance but for survival.

THE POLITICAL AND MILITARY SETTING

Ibn Tulun departed Samarra for Egypt at a critical moment in the history of the Arab-Islamic Empire. Founded in the wake of the seventh-century Arab conquests, the empire had at one time stretched from Iberia (Spain) and the western reaches of North Africa across Egypt and the Near East to eastern Iran and northern India.

The first Arab-Islamic dynasty to govern the vast territory was the Umayyad house (661–750). It laid the groundwork for two far-reaching developments: the Islamization of Iberia, North Africa, the Near East, and Central Asia, and the Arabization of many though not all of these same regions. The two currents, though distinct, interlocked on many levels. The result – the dissemination of Islam and the spread of Arab culture, notably the Arabic language, and its literary and scientific traditions – transformed the course of Mediterranean and Eurasian history. The conversion to Islam by pagans, Jews, Christians, Zoroastrians, and members of other faith communities took place at different rates and for different reasons. Egypt, a majority Christian land, may not have become principally Muslim until the fourteenth century. Historians argue this point: some insist that the threshold to a Muslim majority was crossed much earlier. The adoption of the Arabic language and literature, particularly poetry, and the cross-pollination of Arab culture and science with the cultural patterns of the Mediterranean and Eurasian worlds took less time. Documents from early Islamic Egypt indicate that Greek, Coptic, and Hebrew, the languages of pre-seventh-century Christian Egypt, gave ground to Arabic early on. The latter emerged as the language of commerce, government and, eventually, daily expression.

The Umayyads, for all their achievements, finally let slip their hold on power. A violent mid-eighth-century coup, sprung from southern Iraq and Khurasan, the enormous stretch of eastern Iran, swept the family aside. A new Arab dynasty, the Abbasid house, took its place (see Map 1). The Abbasids relied for long decades on a flourishing agrarian and commercial economy, a well-integrated military, and a lively urban culture. The first caliphs governed well, and the empire enjoyed roughly a century of relative stability. But the puzzles of ruling an unwieldy realm remained. Civil war followed the death of the fifth Abbasid caliph, the storied Harun al-Rashid, in 809. The empire would survive this one round of internecine violence though in much altered form. But the seeds were sown: the great Arab-Islamic empire would give way, by the first part of the tenth century, to regionalism and political fragmentation.

The civil war ended only in 819 with the arrival in Baghdad of Abd Allah al-Ma'mun (r. 813–833). Hard-nosed and cerebral, al-Ma'mun was perhaps the most controversial of the Abbasid caliphs. Having gained prominence as governor of Khurasan, he used his office to challenge the seated caliph, his brother al-Amin. A first phase of war ended with the latter's murder in 813: al-Ma'mun's troops beheaded the unlucky caliph along a sandy bank of the Tigris. The shock of regicide haunted the ruling house from that point on. Through luck, diplomacy, and the backing of leading military families, chief among them the Tahirid clan, al-Ma'mun returned central authority to the imperial office and regained the unity of the realm. To secure Egypt, a wealthy and strategically well-placed province, al-Ma'mun even campaigned there in person in 832, a year before his death. (He was one of only two sitting caliphs to visit Egypt prior to the thirteenth century.)

Al-Amin's murder and the near loss of key provinces, including Egypt, were but the most obvious costs of the war. Longer-term costs had a more subtle effect. So, for example, the caliphate now vested its military and security forces with ever-greater authority. No empire can exist without the capacity to defend its borders and crush domestic opposition. The Abbasids were no exception. The family, after all, owed its ascendance to armed rebellion, and Baghdad, the great imperial center, was constructed in good part to house its regiments. But the extent to which the imperial house turned to repression was new. It seems unsurprising, in this light, that al-Ma'mun was succeeded by his forceful brother, Abu Ishaq al-Mu'tasim (r. 833–842). The latter's success had much to do with a brawny personal style and tight relations with the imperial command.

To bolster the strength of the caliphate, the two men experimented with a new-style military body. The new force consisted of Turkic and Central Asian recruits brought into the Near East from beyond its eastern borders. These men were acquired by the Abbasid state from Central Asian slave traders or seized directly; a smaller number were purchased in Baghdad. They were then pressed into service as commanders and elite fighters and, it seems, subsequently manumitted and converted. Ibn Tulun's father, Tulun, was among the first of these young bonded soldiers.

The recruitment and arming of enslaved and freed persons was not new to the Near East and neighboring regions; the Roman Empire had done so in previous centuries and similar practice can be found in Chinese and Central Asian history. Historians continue to debate how the practice played out in the early Abbasid era. Its first appearance under the Abbasids may have been in North Africa with its use, in this case of African recruits, by the Aghlabids, a long-standing governing family. The idea of exploiting the populations of Iran and Central Asia for this purpose likely came first to al-Ma'mun and his circle. It can be seen as one of that caliph's impetuous policies. The earliest reference, from Ibn Qutayba (d. 889), a ninth-century Iraqi scholar, is direct: al-Ma'mun and his advisors introduced the new force but turned its command over to his younger brother, Abu Ishaq. On taking office as caliph, the latter shaped the units into a formidable army.

Following his accession to office in 833 – and adoption of the regnal title al-Muʿtasim ("the guarantor of God") – the Turkic-Central Asian military emerged as a mainstay of the imperial state.

A second, longer-term effect of the civil war concerned the standing of the caliphate. Despite efforts by al-Ma'mun and his supporters to boost the prestige of the office, it never fully recovered from the war. Caliphs – Umayyad and Abbasid – had always faced opposition. What imperial house does not? Opponents to the caliphate typically expressed themselves in religious form: they connected Abbasid misrule, as they saw it, to the dynasty's impiety. But the civil conflict of 809–833 raised questions of Abbasid legitimation as never before. The killing of al-Amin, though not the first instance of regicide in Islamic history, nonetheless sent a message: Abbasid caliphs were disposable.

The standing of the ruling house also suffered as rising social elites, particularly in Muslim urban quarters, asserted forms of authority largely independent of the caliphate. Such was the case of the religious establishment, represented by legal scholars and their supporters in Baghdad and other prominent cities. These men, representing different strands of Islam, were closely tied to merchant and other elite circles in Iraq, Syria, Khurasan, and North Africa. Interaction with the imperial state was both necessary and practical. After all, the caliphate offered investment opportunities and high-level patronage. But the prestige of the caliphate had slipped. If, in earlier decades, the caliph's office seemed inviolable, it was certainly no longer, and religious leaders was all too happy to step up.

But, again, decline occurred at a gradual pace. Al-Muʿtasim – a commanding figure – proved a worthy heir to his brother. Bringing muscle to the caliphate, he consolidated imperial authority over the provinces. The empire thus regained its feet for decades to come. Egypt, as always, was of particular concern. Al-Muʿtasim, prior to his ascent to office, had served as its governor. In that capacity, in 829–830, he led the Turkic-Central Asian units against a rebellion in the Nile Delta. One early source describes the army as four thousand strong. It is likely that their number included Tulun, Ahmad ibn Tulun's father. If so, he was the first member of the family to see the Nile. More will be said further on about the Turkic military. Suffice it here to say that al-Mu'tasim's campaign introduced the Turkic command to the province. In the later ninth century, nearly all governors and many subordinate officeholders in Egypt were drawn from these same circles. It was as deputy of one such commander that Ibn Tulun – himself a mid-ranked Turkic officer – would arrive in Egypt.

Al-Mu'tasim, once in office, arrived at a far-reaching decision of his own. It was driven by the need to accommodate the Turkic-Central Asian regiments and a growing bureaucratic state. Following a hostile response to the presence of the Turkic units in Baghdad, the new caliph broke ground for a new capital at Samarra, located north along the Tigris River (see Map 1). Samarra replaced Baghdad as the Abbasid capital for some fifty years (836–892), although it never gained the commercial, cultural and intellectual prestige of the older city. The ruin fields of Samarra – stretching for kilometers outside the modern Iraqi city bearing the same name – attest to the size and wealth of al-Mu'tasim's new center. But Samarra, following several decades of dynamic growth, became the venue of a devastating cycle of civil war. Internecine conflict, reopening old wounds, tore at the empire and further undercut Abbasid authority.

At least two factors fed the new conflict. The first concerned the Turkic-Central Asian military command. Wooed by the Abbasids, these men gained lucrative political and economic interests in the years following al-Mu'tasim's reign. The commanders, anxious to defend their interests, finally stepped in to exert direct control over the Abbasid court and, thus, imperial decision-making. The effort saw the violent removal of five caliphs, three of whom fell to military assassins. The humiliation of the Abbasid house was thorough. But the upheaval took a toll as well on the Turkic command itself, as cliques of officers and their supporters turned on one another. (Samarra remained an unhappy place for the Abbasid family and, thus, when opportunity allowed, the imperial house would return to Baghdad at the close of the ninth century.)

The second factor was an extended revolt across southern Iraq. Known usually as the Zanj Rebellion (869–883), it consumed the resources of the caliphate. The Zanj, a population of largely East African slaves and freedmen, backed by local Arab tribesmen, took up arms around 869 in southern Iraq. Their leader, Ali ibn Muhammad (d. 883), an obscure figure, promoted a chameleon-like program that mixed claims to prophecy and descent from the Prophet's family. Modern historians often treat the event in isolation, seeing it as a reaction to the horrific labor conditions to which the Zanj were subjected. Al-Tabari (d. 923), a contemporary historian writing in Arabic, was well placed in Baghdad to observe these developments. He describes their work in reclaiming salt flats for cultivation near the Shatt al-Arab outside Basra. The rebellion endured fifteen years and ran up enormous human and fiscal costs. The Zanj fighters defended the southern Iraqi marshes against Abbasid troops and, on at least one occasion, sacked Basra, a busy commercial hub. (It seems that the Samarran Turkic military, a heavy mounted army, struggled to subdue the Zanj, a small-scale guerrilla force well accustomed to conditions in the marshlands.)

The combination of internecine violence in the capital and the prolonged rebellion had a predictable impact on the stability of the empire. As the grip of the central administration loosened, opportunity arose for a variety of local actors. Governors, warlords, rural clan elders, and religious firebrands in a variety of provinces: all asserted themselves in ways unimaginable had the imperial state stood on firmer ground. The politics of the period – conducted typically at sword's edge and thus unpredictable – bred opportunism at every level.

IBN TULUN AND ABBASID POLITICS

Such was the context for Ibn Tulun's career. What follows here is a brief account of that career; the many details come later.

He arrived in al-Fustat, the Arab-Islamic center of Egypt, located at the southern end of the Nile Delta, precisely at the moment of the worst violence in Samarra and on the eve of the Zanj Rebellion. Each of the two developments would shape his tenure in complex fashion. But what of his appointment? There is reason to suppose that contemporary observers were puzzled by the choice of Ibn Tulun for an office of such prestige. There is little evidence of prior administrative experience or high military command on his part. His formal position was that of resident governor (Ar., *khalifa*), charged with the day-to-day running of the province. He initially governed Egypt, in other words, as agent or deputy of the men who appointed him.

These individuals represented the Abbasid state, at least in principle. The first to appoint Ibn Tulun was Bayakbak (d. 870), a Samarran Turkic commander and, as the appointment indicates, the titular governor of Egypt. He is reported to have chosen Ibn Tulun, again, in 868, on hearing of the latter's piety and acumen. And Ibn Tulun's responsibilities, at first, were limited to military and administrative matters. These involved only al-Fustat and its hinterlands: he had no say over Alexandria, for example, or areas to the immediate west of Egypt. Nor did he have jurisdiction over Egypt's finances. Responsibility for the collection and disbursement of tax and other forms of revenue lay with Ahmad ibn al-Mudabbir (d. 883), the finance director, and his cadre of administrators.

Ibn Tulun quickly rocked the boat, first, in wresting Egypt's fiscal administration away from Ibn al-Mudabbir then, these resources in hand, expanding many-fold the size of his military. He also took strides to unify what was still a fractious land; Egypt, like other provinces, had yet to submit fully to imperial control as will be shown later. Suffice it here to say that Ibn Tulun and his inner circle found much room to pursue local and regional aims. These achievements included the creation of a governing house: Ibn Tulun was succeeded to office by his son, Abu al-Jaysh Khumarawayh (r. 884–896), two grandsons (Jaysh and Harun) and, for a brief moment, another son (Shayban). His success in creating a provincial ruling house points to the inability of the imperial state to exert its will even over such a valuable province as Egypt.

But there is much to suggest that Ibn Tulun and his successors overplayed their hand. An Abbasid expeditionary force finally would destroy the Tulunid state in 905. This was forty years after Ibn Tulun's arrival in al-Fustat and only twenty-one years after his passing. Relative to later Islamic dynasties in Egypt, the duration of the Tulunid period was brief. The violence of the Abbasid assault says much of the contro-versy surrounding Ibn Tulun and his house.

That Ibn Tulun was a dynamic actor is not in question. Muslim-Arabic and Coptic sources laud him for bringing stability and pros-perity to the province. In unifying Egypt, he likely produced a climate favorable to agrarian production and commercial investment. Ibn al-Daya, author of the earliest surviving biography of Ibn Tulun, tells us that he left a considerable fortune to his heir (Khumarawayh), one of a number of indications of Tulunid wealth. Written accounts also make much of Ibn Tulun's success in achieving law and order in what had been an unruly province. This might explain reports that Egyptians – Muslims, Jews, and Christians alike – grieved as one on news of Ibn Tulun's demise in 884. The groundswell of sentiment speaks of a pop-ular standing of which the caliphs in Samarra were likely envious.

But if he governed well in Egypt, his conduct in Syria proved less fortunate. On three occasions, Ibn Tulun led forces north in an effort to expand his territorial reach. The first of these actions ended abruptly, but on two subsequent campaigns he marched deep into Syria as far as the Abbasid-Byzantine frontier.

The sources have it that Ibn Tulun sought to play his part in fight-ing the Byzantine Empire. The Byzantine (or Eastern Roman) Empire had been defeated by the Arab-Islamic forces in the seventh century and driven from Egypt and its other Near Eastern provinces. Firmly rooted in Anatolia, the Byzantines remained a chief antagonist of the Islamic world through the medieval period. It became, in other words, an appropriate target for *jihad*. Roughly translated as "religious war," *jihad* had long historic roots in Near Eastern-Islamic history, providing caliphs and other political figures with a potent source of legitimation. Ibn Tulun learned the lesson early on. But he seems to have misread his ability to turn territorial expansion, including activity on the frontier, to his advantage. He led his troops twice into Syria and to the frontier. On both occasions, the populace of Tarsus, a cen-ter of frontier-style military and religious activity, turned against the governor. (It was in the midst of the second confrontation in Tarsus that Ibn Tulun contracted the illness from which he would die several months later.)

The Syrian campaigns were but a piece of a larger puzzle: Ibn Tulun's relations with the Abbasid center. These relations were ambiguous from the start and, again, make it difficult to pigeonhole his career. It is true that Ibn Tulun confronted his Abbasid overlords; strained relations with Iraq colored much of his policy-making. But Ibn Tulun nurtured ties to at least two caliphs, al-Musta`in (r. 862–866) and al-Mu`tamid (r. 870–892). It was, in part, his determination to support the latter ruler, who was then under considerable pressure, that Ibn Tulun marched into Syria on his last campaign. This went hand-in-hand with his efforts to influence political developments in Iraq.

Ibn Tulun's relations with the Abbasid house were shaped to a large extent by his confrontation with Abu Ahmad al-Muwaffaq (d. 891). An Abbasid prince with close ties to the military brass, al-Muwaffaq gained wide authority in fighting the Zanj. He also proved to be a more decisive figure than his brother, the seated caliph and Ibn Tulun's ally at court, al-Mu`tamid. Capitalizing on his military connections and his brother's relative timidity, al-Muwaffaq effectively ran the imperial state. In this context, his hostility towards Ibn Tulun is unsurprising. The *amir* not only refused to extend expressions of humility and loyalty, but also tightened his grip on Egypt's wealth at a point when the costs of the Zanj war were mounting.

A key to unpacking Ibn Tulun's career lies here. The confrontation with al-Muwaffaq was not simply a struggle over Egypt but for influence over the caliphate as well. Ibn Tulun was a product of the history and politics of Samarra: this is a point to be stressed. The Turkic-Central Asian military command had insinuated itself into imperial decision-making in the years leading up to his departure for Egypt. The effort led Turkic commanders, in a brief spasm of violence, to even turn their weapons on the Samarran caliphs. But they appear never to have considered a claim on the caliphate proper. Rather, it was a matter of tying their futures to the fortunes of the Abbasid house: far better than going it alone. The idea was to keep the unhappy monarchs on the throne but, when necessary, guide them firmly in their decision-making. Ibn Tulun absorbed that very lesson. Born and raised in the imperial center, Ibn Tulun made a point, as an actor of influence and means, to play by Samarran rules.

GOVERNING ABBASID EGYPT

Egypt, the northeast corner of Africa, was ever graced with size, strategic location, and wealth, commercial and agrarian alike. The Nile River is its principal feature, a source of boundless fresh water and a mostly reliable corridor of travel, pilgrimage, trade, and transportation. But nearly as significant to Egypt's history were the arid desert to the west, the Red Sea to the east, and the Mediterranean to the north. These constituted interlocking natural boundaries. As Petra Sijpesteijn has put it, in her study of Islamic Egypt, the "formidable barricade of desert and sea" marked Egypt as "one of the region's most coherent and stable geographical entities."

Egypt was, in sum, no ordinary province. A venue of empire-building in the ancient period, the province was later administered from Rome then, with the rise of the Byzantine (or Eastern Roman) imperial state in the fourth century, from Constantinople. Egypt fell to Arab-Islamic rule in the seventh century and was governed by the Umayyads from Damascus and, from the mid-eighth century on, Abbasid Iraq. The Abbasids needed little reminder of the wealth of Egypt: its revenue was second only to that of Iraq, at least into the tenth century. A brief anecdote from a ninth-century source points to perceptions of Egypt roughly contemporary with Ibn Tulun's career. The story has the caliph, Harun al-Rashid, learn that a senior member of the caliphal court, Yahya ibn Fadl al-Barmaki, had acquired a brilliant slave singer, Mukhariq. The caliph, impressed by the latter's abilities, asked to purchase him. The reply, depending on one's reading, was either haughty or teasing: "He is worth nothing less than the annual revenue of Egypt and its great estates!"

Ibn Tulun was certainly not the first of Egypt's governors to absorb the lessons of that wealth. In this sense, one sees continuity in his tenure: he doubtlessly learned much from his predecessors. We might briefly consider three of these individuals.

The first of these men, Abd al-Aziz ibn Marwan, governed Egypt in the mid-Umayyad period. If a very different period in the empire's history, his tenure (685–705) offers insights into the ingredients required in ruling Egypt. Abd al-Aziz rose to office in the context of civil war, a rough parallel with Ibn Tulun's experience roughly two centuries later. The conflict brought his brother, Abd al-Malik (r. 685–705), to power in Syria, the Umayyad stronghold. Allies early on, the two brothers soon feuded, largely over Abd al-Aziz's resistance to his brother's effort to extend control over Egypt. Abd al-Aziz governed the province for two decades largely free of central intervention, without, however, ever denying the ultimate authority of the caliphate. Unlike Ibn Tulun, however, Abd al-Aziz's bid to have his son succeed him failed. Upon his death, his brother – the reigning caliph – appointed his own son, Abd Allah (705–709), as governor.

Was Ibn Tulun aware of Abd al-Aziz's example? No source says as much, but it would seem surprising if he was not. Both men turned to a potent combination of ingredients – ceremony, monument building, and patronage – in their respective bid for authority. It meant, in part, an appeal to poets: both men were lauded in verse for which they no doubt paid handsomely. It meant, too, a consolidation of arms. To establish himself militarily, Abd al-Aziz pursued alliances with Arab tribes recently settled in Egypt, and with whom he already boasted kinship ties. And, like Ibn Tulun many decades later, Abd al-Aziz knew how to build, investing large sums for a new administrative center at Hulwan, south of al-Fustat. His motivation may have been as religious as it was political: Hulwan housed an ancient Egyptian necropolis, and the decision to build there may have been to appeal to local tradition. The project recalls Ibn Tulun's choice of Jabal Yashkur on which to build his new mosque after learning of the religious significance that Egyptians – Jews and Christians – attached to the site.

The decade-long career of Ubayd Allah ibn al-Habhab (724–734) also dates to the Umayyad period. Appointed to head Egypt's fiscal administration, Ibn al-Habhab never actually held the office of governor. His aggressive style – he had two governors dismissed – drew on his vigorous approach to social and fiscal policy, as well as a close relationship with the caliph, Hisham ibn Abd al-Malik (r. 724–743). Two decisions on Ibn al-Habhab's part stood out. First, he raised taxes following a major land survey and, second, he transferred from Syria to the Nile Delta a large Qaysi Arab tribal population. The first decision sparked revolt by Egypt's rural populace against which local imperial forces were dispatched; the second enhanced the Arab-Muslim presence in rural Egypt. No less a feature of Ibn al-Habhab's tenure was the prominence of his sons, Qasim and Isma`il, the first of whom succeeded his father over Egypt's fiscal administration in 734.

Did Ibn Tulun know of Ibn al-Habhab's career? We can only guess. More certain is his knowledge of the career of Yazid ibn Abdallah. Ibn Abdallah governed Egypt for eleven years (856–867), on behalf of four Abbasid caliphs, beginning with al-Mutawakkil (r. 847–861), all of whom fell victim to the violence of Samarra. Ibn Abdallah was thus a close predecessor and so shared a history with Ibn Tulun. For most of the early Abbasid period, governors had rotated through Egypt at a steady clip and thus seldom held office long enough to shape a local power base. Ibn Abdallah, like Ibn Tulun, represented a change: the shift of control of Egypt to the Samarran Turkish military, a shift that led, of course, to Ibn Tulun's own appointment. Ibn Abdallah carried out several measures that look familiar. He clamped down on local Alids, for example, and their followers. ("Alid" signifies members and partisans of the family of Ali ibn Abi Talib, the cousin, son-in-law, and eventual successor of the Prophet in the first years of Islam.) Ibn Abdallah also enacted a number of fiscal and administrative measures, including, it seems, the construction of a new Nilometer (Ar., *miqyas*), the gauge used to measure the annual rise of the great river. He confronted, however, a serious revolt, led by Arab tribal chiefs in alliance with Ibn al-Arqat (about whom more will be said later). Despite the concerted effort of imperial forces, Ibn Abdallah failed to bring lasting order to the Egyptian countryside. That task would fall to Ibn Tulun. His success in that regard was a significant step in his rise to prominence.

Ibn Tulun's predecessors were thus individuals of considerable standing and ambition. What set Ibn Tulun apart was the extent of his authority. This is to see that Ibn Tulun succeeded where these earlier governors did not. It goes far, of course, in explaining the controversy that surrounded his tenure. Here the point is that to govern Egypt was to wield considerable human and natural resources. The trick was to govern well. One had to appreciate Egypt's unique geography and know how best to manage its river system, vast estates, commercial markets, and its productive mines. Sound stewardship, in effect, required a sense of proportion. The resources of Egypt could be guarded effectively against outside threat – recall its "barricade" of frontiers – and thus used to remarkable effect in developing the province itself. Such luxury of geography was enjoyed by almost no other region of North Africa and the Near East.

But a sense of proportion was not easily gained. Wealth and authority, across Near Eastern history, never failed to breed a sense of entitlement on the part of Egyptian strongmen. Over and again, they would claim title to neighboring territories. The logic of geography pointed to Palestine and Syria: the Sinai Peninsula offered a corridor to the north. Territorial expansion was a temptation that Ibn Tulun, like other masters of Egypt before and since, was unable to resist. Like them, he proceeded at considerable risk to all that he had accomplished in Egypt itself. It has been suggested already that he overbid his hand. His legacy, a formidable army and ample treasury, allowed his heirs to press on, but for a limited time. The Tulunid dynasty, in effect, fell victim to political hubris, as this book will indicate.

The history of the Tulunid period, measured against the millennia of Near Eastern dynastic history, endured but a moment. Why, then, take an interest in Ibn Tulun's career? It has in part to do with his achievements in governing Egypt. But the answer lies as well in Ibn Tulun's contribution, first, to the unraveling of the last of the ancient Near Eastern empires – the Arab-Islamic state – and, second, the articulation of a new-style Near Eastern politics. His reign was an experiment and, as such, won the interest of medieval historians, essayists, poets, and travelers. It should not be confused for universal admiration: many of the *amir*'s contemporaries applauded the destruction of his regime. But such was the Tulunid venture that no observer could turn his eyes away.

This book, in sum, considers a fascinating public life. Chapters 1 and 2 provide a narrative of Ibn Tulun's tenure in office, set against the context of ninth-century Abbasid politics and society, and with an opening word on the sources of Ibn Tulun's life. Chapter 3 considers the institutions and patterns of conduct on which the *amir* relied in governing Egypt and, fitfully, Syria. Chapter 4 turns to his political and ideological repertoire – the ideas and practices to which Ibn Tulun appealed in ruling his new state. The book closes with a brief chapter on the remaining years of Tulunid rule, with a brief survey of Egypt's history to roughly 969 and the introduction of a new Islamic empire, the Fatimid state. Readers are encouraged to use the maps and other images for a visual sense of the context in which Ibn Tulun's career played out. A final element is the list of secondary works for those interested in learning more of Ibn Tulun's career and its historical context.

THE FIRST DECADE IN OFFICE
868–877

Several types of sources allow us to reconstruct Ibn Tulun's career. Physical clues lie in coins, glass weights, and other material artifacts. On hand, as well, are a considerable number of documents, most produced on papyrus, many of which have yet to be studied in detail. The documents are particularly helpful as regards Tulunid administrative history. And there is the great mosque itself. But no less a source are written works produced principally in Arabic by scholars from the ninth century on. Egyptian authors, in particular, produced chronicles, biographical dictionaries, and other forms of writing that provide detailed information on Ibn Tulun and his successors. Two authors will be cited often in this study. Muhammad ibn Yusuf al-Kindi (d. 961), about whose career we know little, wrote extensively on Egypt's history, including a chronicle of provincial governors in the early Islamic period, among them Ibn Tulun. Taqi al-Din al-Maqrizi (d. 1442), a remarkably prolific later Egyptian historian, includes much information on Ibn Tulun's career in several of his books.

The main written sources, however, are two biographies of Ibn Tulun, each produced by a scholar of tenth-century Egypt. The two works are closely related in both content and dating. We will refer to them simply as "the two biographies." The *Sira* of al-Balawi, our most important source, was introduced earlier. Abdallah ibn Muhammad al-Balawi was a minor religious scholar of the late tenth century, with probably strong Shi`ite sympathies. The second, earlier work was produced by Ahmad ibn Yusuf ibn Ibrahim. He is often referred to as Ibn al-Daya, and we will do so here as well, although this seems to have been his father's nickname. Ahmad ibn Yusuf is thought to have died only some years before al-Balawi, so likely in the mid- to late 940s. Ibn al-Daya served in the Tulunid administration, probably taking over the office of his father. The latter, Yusuf ibn Ibrahim, had served the Abbasids in Samarra before moving to Egypt sometime after 839–840.

The two biographers – Ibn al-Daya and al-Balawi – may have been acquainted though no source says as much. We know that Ibn al-Daya wrote a history of the Tulunids. His reason for doing so is unclear. We cannot say for certain if he wrote it on behalf of a Tulunid (or pro-Tulunid) patron. What is clear is that he drew extensively on eyewitness accounts; he names, throughout the book, the individuals from whom he collected information. Most of these informants are known to have served Ibn Tulun or his family directly, usually as members of the wider Tulunid household. The book thus offers glimpses, indistinct, of individuals about whom, otherwise, we would know nothing. There is, for this reason, an immediacy to Ibn al-Daya's account.

Ibn al-Daya appears to have written a full history of the Tulunids. All that remains, however, is the section on Ibn Tulun himself; Ibn al-Daya's account of the later Tulunid period is (so far) missing. The extended fragment, in addition, survives only in a single version contained in a history of Egypt from fourteenth-century Islamic Spain. This poses a problem: how does Ibn al-Daya's book relate to al-Balawi's text, which the latter produced an unknown number of years later? Without the original of Ibn al-Daya to hand, this remains very difficult to answer. But the two biographies are obviously related. Al-Balawi states upfront that he derived much of his information on Ibn Tulun from Ibn al-Daya, and it is clear that he copied much of the earlier text nearly verbatim. Yet al-Balawi insists that he not only developed Ibn al-Daya's material but added new information of his own. His position, needless to say, is that he improved on his colleague's effort. In a long opening statement, he argues that Ibn al-Daya gathered valuable information but had little sense of how to write history. The task thus fell to him to do a better job of treating the topic, that is, the life and career of Ibn Tulun.

This study relies heavily on al-Balawi's *Sira*, and no history of the Tulunids can do otherwise. It is clear that later Egyptian historians, notably al-Maqrizi, used it extensively. It is a long and invaluable account of Ibn Tulun's career. But, to be fair to Ibn al-Daya, it is important to recall again that much of what al-Balawi provides derives from his older colleague: Ibn al-Daya was the wellspring.

The two biographers, Ibn al-Daya and al-Balawi, focus on Ahmad ibn Tulun's years in office, that is, his adult years. Of his youth and upbringing, unfortunately, they offer only a sketch, dealing for the most part with his religious training, relations with his fellow "Turks," as they were known, and the circumstances of his appointment to Egypt.

Ahmad's father, Tulun, was of Central Asian origin. Ninth-century Abbasid society knew him as a *Turk* (pl. *Atrak*). The term, widely used in the medieval Near East for individuals of Turkic and Central Asian background, including the *Atrak* of Abbasid Iraq, masks the fact that they derived from a variety of regions and cultural backgrounds. The Arabic sources often use "*Turk*" in catchall fashion, in other words, and so the origins of a given individual are seldom clear.

Tulun is something of an exception. The biographers report that he entered Abbasid service as a slave. One indication is his single name, presumably assigned to him upon his enslavement. The name may be derived from Turkish (*dolun* = "full moon"), which may reflect nothing more than that his captors knew the language. The single name, in any case, reflects his initial servile standing; the use of such evocative names was common to slave-owning societies across world history. The references add that he was of Toghuz-ghuz origin, a term that medieval Arabic authors typically used for the Uyghurs, a Central Asian people. So, in his case, we do have at least a rough indication of origin.

The biographers add that Tulun was included in an annual tribute of cash, horses, and slaves presented to al-Ma'mun by an Abbasid governor in Khurasan. The year was 815–816. Al-Ma'mun, in his capacity as vice-regent of the vast province, was immersed at that point in civil war against his brother. The formation of the well-known Turkic-Central Asian "slave military" occurred in this context, and Tulun,

Ahmad's father, is likely to have been an early member. The new units, created by al-Ma'mun, were assigned to his brother, Abu Ishaq (the future caliph, al-Mu'tasim, at that point still a prince). It is likely that Tulun joined al-Ma'mun at the end of the civil war on the new caliph's return to Baghdad in 819. The new military settled in Iraq from that point on.

It seems that Tulun underwent an early change in legal standing. It is impossible to tell when, though certainly before Ibn Tulun's birth. One clue comes in reference to Ahmad's mother. The biographers refer to her as Qasim (though some later sources read her name as Hashim). The single name, like Tulun, is one indication that she too was enslaved: "Qasim," a typical male name, was perhaps assigned her in jest. Unfortunately, the sources say nothing direct about her name, origins, and ultimate legal standing. There is wide evidence in contemporary sources regarding the scale of the ninth-century Near Eastern slave trade. It is difficult to pin down hard numbers, but there is good reason to think that a majority was made up of girls and young women. Many likely ended up in urban households as domestic workers or, in other cases, as concubines of their male owners. The women were of a great variety of ethnic and geographic origin including Central Asia and the Turkic steppe. It is only a guess that Qasim shared Tulun's Turkic background. On this question, regrettably, the sources are silent.

Ibn al-Daya indicates that Qasim bore Tulun four children: Ahmad, Musa (his difficult brother about whom more will be said later), and two sisters (about whom nothing is known apart from their names, Habsiya and Samana). The relationship of mother and father, however, is difficult to characterize. A likely option is that Qasim was Tulun's concubine. This suggests the shift in Tulun's legal standing: Islamic law typically allowed free Muslim males to own concubines but denied male slaves the same right. It is reasonable to think that Tulun was manumitted at some point following his entry into Abbasid military service. As a freedman, he then legally acquired Qasim or, perhaps, was offered her as a gift. Gifting slave women was a common gesture in Abbasid circles. A second option is that they were husband and wife: Islamic law generally allowed slaves to marry, in which case

Tulun did not own Qasim. But, of this option, there are no clear indications. There are also no indications that Tulun ever acquired another concubine (or married a second time).

Of Tulun's career, there is indirect evidence that he advanced in rank. He served the imperial army for many years, so some manner of promotion seems unremarkable. This suggests, in turn, that he and his offspring enjoyed a certain standing in Samarran military society; the Tulunid household was one with which others sought to associate, whether through marriage or some other means. The suggestion, in other words, is that young Ahmad was raised in a house of local prestige. One indication comes in the reference to Tulun's closest companions. Following Tulun's death, they are reported to have devoted themselves to seeing to the interests of his two sons, Ahmad and Musa.

Ahmad – the subject of this book – was born in 835, the eldest, it seems, of his parents' offspring. The site of his birth was Baghdad: the Turkic-Central Asian military, along with the Abbasid ruling family, the imperial administration, and a large civilian population, only moved to Samarra after 838, following the city's foundation by al-Muʿtasim several years earlier. Less easy to identify is Ahmad's legal standing at birth. Tulun and Qasim had entered Abbasid society as slaves, and if they had retained that standing, their children were born into slavery. The question turns on Tulun's standing. Islamic law typically assigned children the same standing as the father; if he was free and acknowledged paternity which, it seems, Tulun was and did, then his offspring were considered free persons as well. But, again, his (Tulun's) standing remains unclear, and the sources do note that he was twenty at the time of Ahmad's birth, so a relatively young man. One possibility then is that Ahmad began his life as an enslaved person and underwent manumission at some later date. The sources say nothing on this score.

Samarra was the site of Ahmad's formative years. The Tulunid household was a military one, and the assumption is that Ahmad and his siblings grew up in one of the barrack neighborhoods created in Samarra for the imperial regiments. Modern scholars have identified these neighborhoods in the vast ruin fields in modern-day Iraq. The household was also at least bilingual: Ahmad, his biographers tell us, spoke both Arabic and Turkish and, late in life, enjoyed Turkish-language poetry. It is a shame that so little is known of Qasim's background: if she introduced a third language and its cultural references to her son's formation, the sources do not let on.

Ahmad followed his father into the armed forces. But, curiously, there is almost no information on his induction or training. A passing comment has him on the military payroll; it is but one of very few references to his early professional life (a second reference describes him as a skilled archer). But Ahmad's biographers generally seem disinterested in his experience as a soldier. They are careful, however, to detail his formation as a Muslim. The boy, they tell us, memorized the Qur'an – a typical step for the offspring of devout households – and studied the teachings of the Prophet (Hadith). He did so not only in Samarra but in Tarsus as well. A town on the Islamic/Byzantine frontier, Tarsus was home to circles of scholar-warriors who divided their time between fighting, education, mystical practice, and Qur'anic exegesis. The biographers indicate that Ibn Tulun traveled often to Tarsus to study with these men. He earned, in the process, a reputation for piety and purpose.

What to make of the special interest in Ibn Tulun's religious formation? The two biographers craft an image of the *amir* as a sober, properly motivated figure, and al-Balawi, in particular, insists that Ibn Tulun was committed to Islamic principles throughout his career. The point no doubt carried much weight for these Muslim writers and their medieval peers. We return later to this effort to represent the governor as meeting the highest standards of personal and public conduct. But was it simply an exercise in image making? It seems not; there is much to suggest that the governor's devotion to the faith was genuine. His construction of a large-scale mosque can be cited as evidence. So, too, the many indications that Ibn Tulun retained close interest in developments on the Abbasid/Byzantine frontier. He would devote much of his later career to securing a presence in Tarsus and its environs.

But al-Balawi also refers to behavior on Ibn Tulun's part that, to modern sensibilities, might seem unbecoming. That the *amir* had to negotiate the currents of hard imperial politics seems clear; the effort hardly allowed for strict adherence to principle. But perhaps a better way to approach the question is to see that a reputation for religious mindedness served one well in ninth-century Iraq. It would have had particular resonance for a rising star of a minority community. The first-generation Turkic-Central Asian soldiers, Tulun among them, had arrived as outsiders to Abbasid imperial society generally and Iraqi urban society specifically. None, in all likelihood, were Muslims upon their arrival and there are many indications that they were perceived as rough outsiders. Iraqi sources describe the young recruits as having settled uneasily in Baghdad in the period prior to the founding of Samarra; they refer specifically to repeated clashes with the local populace. (The hostility generated by their presence, as noted earlier, was a chief reason for al-Mu`tasim's decision to depart Baghdad.)

Given this environment, Ibn Tulun's parents may well have sought out the best routes to integration, for themselves and their offspring. A demonstrated commitment to the dominant faith would have played well. This is to see Ibn Tulun as having received a sound religious training, and as having acted frequently on that basis. But it is also to suggest something about Ibn Tulun's ambitions. At what point did these take hold? It is hard to tell. But a reputation for right-mindedness would no doubt have been useful in negotiating Abbasid society. His biographers, in treating Ibn Tulun's early years, make much of the connection between religious devotion and political success.

Ibn al-Daya and al-Balawi do so, for example, in describing Ibn Tulun's quick rise up the ranks of the Samarran military. And, here, another question arises. Ibn al-Daya and al-Balawi indicate that the young Ibn Tulun chafed at the irreligious ways of his fellow Turkic soldiers. Ibn al-Daya is blunt: Ibn Tulun grew tired of his peers making light of Islamic ritual duties. The references are vague; it is impossible to know whether his reaction grew from a specific event, perhaps the brawls in the streets of Baghdad. The point is that Ibn Tulun distanced himself from his own community. Together with a close companion – Ahmad ibn Muhammad ibn Khaqan al-Wasiti – he applied for transfer to Tarsus from the vizier, Ubayd Allah ibn Yahya (d. 877). The latter presided at that point over the court of the caliph al-Mutawakkil. If the episode took place as described, it was perhaps the first occasion in which Ibn Tulun drew the notice of imperial overlords.

It is the only reference to Ibn Tulun's inclusion on the military rosters: the two men asked for a transfer to the frontier rolls. The request granted, the two men moved to Tarsus where they resided for some unstated period of time. The biographers describe Ibn Tulun as having formed deep ties to the frontier city and its ethos of ascetic warfare. Tarsus thus became, after Samarra, the second of three cultural settings in which Ibn Tulun established himself. The third setting, of course, would be Egypt. These are merely hints, but they point to an uneasy mix of qualities on the young officer's part: an ability to accommodate to new circumstances but a certain restlessness as well.

To sum up briefly, only piecemeal information exists on Ibn Tulun's early years. The biographers provide useful tidbits yet leave many questions unanswered. One such question concerns the extent to which Ibn Tulun took part in campaigning against the Byzantines. The sources say nothing on this score; it remains uncertain, for example, if and when Ibn Tulun took part in actual combat. Related is the question of Ibn Tulun's ties to his Turkic and Central Asian peers in Samarra. The biographers say that he found their company intolerable; however, it is clear that he gained lasting support from within their ranks, and went on to sustain relationships of this kind over the course of his career. We return to both questions shortly.

And there is this question: how might Ibn Tulun have identified himself if asked? It seems right to suppose that he saw himself as a literate and devout Muslim, a free man, the offspring of a bi- (and possibly tri-) lingual military household, a soldier by training, an imperial servant by appointment, and an Abbasid loyalist. Would he have spoken of his mother? He might, but in private; in public such information is likely to have been seen as inappropriate. The medieval sources, at any rate, seldom delve into details of family and domestic life. And what of his parents' servile origins? Was it a subject of conversation? And did it have an effect on Ibn Tulun's rise to prominence? His biographers, sadly, leave off discussion of this kind. On another topic, however, they prove to be more generous: the events leading to his official departure for Egypt.

THE APPOINTMENT TO EGYPT

Ibn Tulun turned twenty in 854. His whereabouts at this point are difficult to pin down, but there is reason to think that he was on the frontier when word arrived of his father's death. A brief anecdote has Ibn Tulun's mother bemoan her eldest son's absence from Samarra. His frontier companions, including al-Wasiti, responded by pressing Ibn Tulun to attend to his familial duties: "your chosen path [i.e., participation in frontier holy war] is for those who are unattached." Ever responsible, Ibn Tulun prepared to return to Iraq.

Events, however, took an unexpected turn. Ibn Tulun joined a trade caravan headed south; alongside merchants, other civilians, and a small armed guard, the caravan included an Abbasid envoy. The latter figure, probably an elite eunuch, had in hand a shipment of precious goods purchased surreptitiously from Byzantine markets for the reigning caliph, al-Musta`in (r. 862–866). These were luxury items, available only in Byzantium; the caliph apparently was skirting public opinion if not imperial regulation in acquiring such goods from the perennial enemy. In Syria, according to al-Balawi, Arab tribal riders robbed the caravan. Ibn Tulun acted promptly: he chased down the raiders, all while demonstrating prowess with sword and bow, and recovered the stolen goods including the mule bearing the caliph's treasure. (This is nearly the only reference to Ibn Tulun wielding arms; the sources perhaps decided not to associate him with activity normal to those of "lesser station," that is, his fellow Turks and other rank-and-file soldiers.)

There is much about the account – the reason for Ibn Tulun's return to Iraq and his rescue of the caliph's ill-gotten property – that is contrived. The attempt to contrast the two figures, for example, seems obvious: the rightly guided imperial servant (Ibn Tulun) and the morally wayward Abbasid caliph (al-Musta`in). The story seems to play, in other words, with the issue of what constituted proper claims to leadership. But, more to the point, the story seems designed to prepare us for Ibn Tulun's appointment to Egypt. It turns next to Ibn Tulun's encounter with al-Musta`in, one of two Abbasid monarchs with whom he enjoyed close relations. (The second caliph, al-Mu'tamid, will make his appearance later.) It is important to recall the backdrop to these relationships, which was the violent intervention by the Samarran military command in the affairs of the imperial court.

The Abbasid envoy, upon returning to Samarra, wasted no time in describing Ibn Tulun's heroics to al-Musta'in. The caliph offered Ibn Tulun a cash reward and, in a gesture typical of elite Abbasid culture, the gift of a young slave woman, Mayyas ("Graceful" is a rough translation). We should note, again, the assignment of a suggestive (and male) name to an enslaved young woman. The first of at least several concubines in Ibn Tulun's possession, Mayyas would give birth in Samarra to his son and heir, Abu al-Jaysh Khumarawayh. Was this effectively a reprise of the moment when Tulun (his father) gained possession of Qasim (his mother) decades earlier? The sources do not say so directly. But the reference is useful on another count as it indicates that Ibn Tulun was either free or a freedman at this point since, typically, Islamic law forbade slaves from owning property including persons. Also, it is significant that Ibn Tulun, perhaps like his father, was a slave owner in his own right. In this he joined urban society at large; slave ownership was a routine feature of Abbasid society, and nothing of either man's possession of concubines likely stood out.

The account of Ibn Tulun's appointment to Egypt begins to take shape. The caliph, recognizing Ibn Tulun as a potential ally, pursued relations with the charismatic young officer. But he did so cautiously, the sources tell us, so as not to draw the unwelcome attention of more senior Turkic-Central Asian officers. Al-Musta'in's anxieties regarding these men were well founded. In 866, shortly after Ibn Tulun's return from Tarsus, commanders replaced the caliph with a more pliable candidate, al-Mu'tazz (r. 866–869). They then exiled the dethroned ruler to the southern Iraqi city of Wasit, assigning Ibn Tulun as his escort. They did so, the biographers explain, out of admiration for the young officer's high-minded character. His treatment of the exiled al-Musta'in only burnished his reputation; he is said to have accorded the former caliph every comfort while maintaining proper deference. Ibn Tulun, we are told, allowed the exiled monarch to hunt, a prerogative of the Near Eastern monarch.

A new test of Ibn Tulun's mettle followed. The commanders supporting al-Mu'tazz were close allies of Qabiha, the new caliph's concubine mother. Suspicious of the dethroned al-Musta'in, she feared an attempt at his reinstatement, and thus the ouster of al-Mu'tazz. She and her Turkic military allies decided on al-Musta'in's assassination. Qabiha wrote to Ibn Tulun offering an appointment over Wasit in exchange for the exiled monarch's head. His reply was immediate: "By God, He, the All-Mighty, will not see me slaughter a caliph to whom I have sworn the oath of allegiance and sacred trust!" The reminder is of Ibn Tulun's sense of duty and right. But the deed was decided: the commanders turned to Sa'id al-Hajib, a ranking civilian official, who acted promptly and in person. Sa'id returned to Samarra as quickly as he arrived, the ex-caliph's head in hand. It fell to Ibn Tulun to bury al-Musta'in's remains. In al-Balawi's account, he weeps over the ruined body.

The story is strained: one would think it sensible for the Turkic-Central Asian command to destroy Ibn Tulun as well. He defied direct orders, in effect, by not carrying out the execution. But something else happened. His duties no longer required, Ibn Tulun returned to the capital to wide acclaim over his determination to uphold the oath of allegiance to a (once) seated caliph. The biographers – here al-Balawi – drive the point home, saying, "When Ibn Tulun wrote of his decision [not to execute al-Musta'in], he captured the hearts of the Turks as never before. They praised his strength of purpose and excellence of conduct." His stance no doubt also appealed to wider political circles in Samarra, certainly in any case the supporters of the deposed caliph.

This is an appropriate place to return to the question of Ibn Tulun's relations with his Samarran peers. He decried their conduct, as seen earlier, but nonetheless his Turkic peers embraced him. One explanation is to see that Ibn Tulun had ties to specific military circles in Samarra. This is borne out by references to his warm relations with his father's closest companions. A way to solve the puzzle, in other words, is to see Ibn Tulun as having come to represent the interests of one element of the Turkic-Central Asian command. It is clear that wide divisions existed in Samarran military society. Iraqi sources, in particular, indicate that the Samarran high command, backed by rank

and file units and civilian officials, was divided by clique and shift-
ing alliance. In this case, it was a matter of those who sided with
al-Mu'tazz, Qabiha, and their allies, and those supporting al-Musta'in,
among them Ibn Tulun. This is to argue that it was the latter circle
that celebrated Ibn Tulun's righteous behavior and, over many years,
supported his rise to prominence.

Ibn Tulun's appointment to Egypt occurred shortly after his return
to Samarra. The Abbasid house had taken to the practice of selecting
allies – military men and civilians – as vice-regents. Such individuals were appointed over entire divisions of the empire, encompassing
often several regions at once. It fell to these appointees to then dele-
gate authority over each province. The vice-regents, in other words,
remained in the capital, unburdened by the strains of day-to-day provincial administration.

The individual in this case was Bayakbak (or, as some Arabic sources
have it, Bakbak). Al-Mu'tazz, seeking to strengthen his position, had
recently placed Bayakbak, a member of the Turkic-Central Asian
command, over Egypt and other western provinces. The sources,
sadly, say little about Bayakbak's background and career. As things
turned out, his pre-eminence proved short-lived. In 869, he fell victim to the internecine bloodletting that decimated the ranks of the
Samarran military. Bayakbak's disgrace and violent death was orches-
trated by al-Musta'in's first cousin, the caliph al-Muhtadi (r. 869),
working with supporters in the Turkic command following the ouster
of al-Mu'tazz.

Bayakbak was only one in a series of Turkic and Central Asian
military men to win appointment over Egypt. Al-Balawi makes the
point explicitly. The commanders, as vice-regents, appointed younger
protégés from their ranks as deputies. It is these latter men who took
up residence in al-Fustat and the responsibilities of daily administration. Bayakbak's choice, again, was Ibn Tulun; he was, once again,
tapped for a high-level and difficult assignment. The biographies have
Bayakbak come to the decision after hearing descriptions of Ibn Tulun
as a devout and single-minded figure, widely admired in military and
political circles. If there is anything to these reports, it is that Ibn
Tulun continued to draw support from influential allies at court.

Shortly thereafter, age thirty-four, Ibn Tulun departed Iraq. He never returned. Two campaigns in Syria and the Byzantine frontier zone would later have him on the road for some five years in all, but he otherwise remained in Egypt.

He arrived in 868. Al-Balawi refers to a small group of locals, gathered before a modest store, among them a blind sage. As Ibn Tulun rides past, the sage describes him precisely as he had seen the *amir* in a vision; his arrival was predestined. The biographers add that Ibn Tulun entered al-Fustat in Ramadan, an auspicious month on the Islamic calendar, marking as it did the onset of divine revelation to the Prophet in 610 and, thus, from an early point in Islamic tradition, a month of obligatory fasting, contemplation, and social gathering. The intent of such references seems clear; Ibn Tulun was no ordinary appointee, and his arrival marked a happy turn in Egypt's fortunes.

Through luck, force of will, and the support of well-placed allies in Samarra and Egypt, Ibn Tulun would achieve an unprecedented degree of control over the Nile Valley. Was such his initial aim? Or did power fall to him in incremental, even accidental, fashion? Ibn al-Daya largely ignores the question (but, again, only a partial version of his text survives). Al-Balawi, by contrast, makes much of Ibn Tulun's lucky star, noting repeatedly that events, one after the other, worked to the governor's advantage. But he is keen to make the point as well that Ibn Tulun knew to exploit each opportunity. It was a matter of good fortune joined to a determination to pursue aims well beyond those of previous governors.

These aims were three-fold. In his first decade in office (868–877), Ibn Tulun consolidated authority over the imperial administration of Egypt. This entailed control over the security, intelligence, and fiscal offices of the province, which typically did not fall to the governor. Second, he brought a new level of order to a still divided Egypt, extending the authority of al-Fustat across the province. It was an effort at greater centralization over the Nile Valley and, eventually, regions lying outside its borders. And, finally, Ibn Tulun pursued new-style relations with the Abbasid house. He achieved the first and second goals within that same ten-year period. The result, again, was unprecedented authority over Egypt. And, in asserting himself in this manner, he acquired new prominence on the imperial stage. The third goal, however, proved more elusive.

THE CLAIM TO FULL AUTHORITY

In 868 Ibn Tulun arrived in a province long integrated into the Arab-Islamic Empire. He thus inherited from his predecessors – notably Yazid ibn Abdallah al-Turki, in office from 856–866 – long-established fiscal and administrative structures. Initial steps had Ibn Tulun reach out to the ranking members of three significant offices: the *shurta*, or local police and security forces; the *barid*, the intelligence and postal system; and the *diwan al-kharaj*, the main finance bureau. Al-Kindi, the early Egyptian historian, reports that Ibn Tulun retained a certain Bulghiya (or Bughya) as head of the *shurta* for a short while before replacing him with Buzan al-Turki. The names strongly suggest that both men were of Samarran military origin; their role in local administration, in turn, points to the presence of a standing Samarran force in Egypt at the point of Ibn Tulun's arrival.

Of equal interest is Ibn Tulun's encounter with the other two ranking members of Egypt's civilian government. The two men are said to have been on hand to welcome Ibn Tulun upon his arrival in al-Fustat: Shuqayr (d. 871), head of the *barid*, and Ahmad ibn al-Mudabbir (d. 883), the finance director. Neither man enjoyed much local support. They were, after all, the chief agents of the Abbasid state, charged with imposing imperial fiat upon the province. The Egyptian populace, in the Umayyad period and now under the Abbasids, had proved, time and again, deeply resistant. Expressed in a variety of forms, the resistance issued from both the majority Christian (Coptic) populace and the ever-larger numbers of Muslim Arab inhabitants of Egypt, many descended from the original settlers of the conquest era.

Such was the context in which both officials worked. But each man enjoyed the prestige of high office and could call on the backing of the Abbasid state if and when trouble arose. Ibn Tulun was the newcomer, though it is likely that he could draw on the support of the local military command in Egypt. His quick efforts to oust Shuqayr

and Ibn al-Mudabbir suggests, of course, the extent of his early ambition. They made for good press needless to say and his biographers
oblige with lively anecdotes.

Shuqayr was evidently the easier target. The biographies identify
him as a freedman (Ar., *ghulam*), previously owned by Qabiha, the
mother of al-Mu'tazz and a busy participant in Samarran court politics. Ahmad ibn Abi Ya'qub al-Ya'qubi (d. c. 897), another early
historian, provides further information. Al-Ya'qubi, as a one-time
Tulunid finance official, was likely well informed on developments
in Egypt, and his chronicle, the *Ta'rikh* (*History*), provides welcome
details on the Tulunid period. Identifying Shuqayr as a eunuch (Ar.,
khadim), he has him in charge of the Egyptian *barid* and in possession
of large estates across the province. Shuqayr, for this reason, comes
over as a local heavyweight, with an abiding interest in Egyptian fiscal
matters and close connections to the imperial court. Ibn Tulun's move
against Shuqayr says much of the new governor's willingness to offend
Abbasid circles.

Matters came to a head following Ibn Tulun's initial encounter
with Shuqayr and Ibn al-Mudabbir. The two men, in separate letters, wrote to the court in Samarra warning of Ibn Tulun's ambitions.
Word of their communication quickly reached the *amir*. Ever alert
to opportunity, Ibn Tulun ordered Shuqayr, described as corpulent,
to hurry by foot to the palace. There, in a less than subtle gesture,
Shuqayr was made to view an array of torture devices. This is the
first of many references to Ibn Tulun's impatient, often cruel, treatment of opponents. The aim was to have Shuqayr succumb to either
exhaustion or dread. It worked: Shuqayr collapsed and died at home
shortly thereafter.

Al-Ya'qubi reports that Ibn Tulun replaced Shuqayr with one
Ahmad ibn al-Husayn al-Ahwazi (about whom little is known). The
passing reference points to a pattern by which Ibn Tulun filled administrative offices on his own rather than automatically accept officials
sent from Iraq. It was a further step in his consolidation of authority.
He now controlled, in the case of the *barid*, official communication
with the imperial court. The office allowed him, as well, to monitor
political developments in al-Fustat and across the province.

If Shuqayr was easily pushed aside, the finance chief, Ibn al-Mudabbir, was a more difficult case. A seasoned political actor, he had long-standing connections in Samarra, among them his brother, Ibrahim (d. 893), a poet and ranking member of Abbasid court society. Ibn al-Mudabbir, prior to his move to Egypt, had served two caliphs previously, al-Wathiq (r. 842–847) and al-Mutawakkil, which further suggests a level of support in the capital. He appears to have distinguished himself in particular under al-Mutawakkil. Al-Ya'qubi, referring to his achievements to that point, comments that he had "increased the flow of revenue considerably."

Ibn al-Mudabbir was thus well situated in al-Fustat. On the heels of a dispute with Ubayd Allah ibn Yahya – the same official to whom Ibn Tulun had sought transfer to the frontier early in his career – Ibn al-Mudabbir had been assigned to Damascus. He was then appointed over Egypt's fiscal administration, in 862, by the short-lived caliph al-Muntasir (r. 861–862). He thus preceded Ibn Tulun in the province by some six years. His dogged approach to office no doubt suited his imperial masters but earned him little local affection. Egyptian sources chide him for a heavy fiscal hand and, specifically, for having imposed arbitrary new taxes. Al-Balawi barely conceals his contempt: Ibn al-Mudabbir was cold-hearted, "a fiend among the high officials." His language falls in line with other evidence regarding Ibn al-Mudabbir's local reputation.

Ibn Tulun turned the controversy to good purpose. The biographers describe an early meeting in which Ibn al-Mudabbir presented Ibn Tulun with expensive gifts. An elaborate bribe, the gifts included fine Egyptian garments, horses, and imported slaves, all valued at a hefty ten thousand dinars. Ibn Tulun dismissed the offer, commenting that he wished nothing from his counterpart. A worried Ibn al-Mudabbir is quoted: "The imperial center might think twice before appointing such a person over one of its provinces – he thinks little of ten thousand dinars!" The *amir* then pressed Ibn al-Mudabbir to surrender a more valuable prize: his personal guard. Ibn al-Daya quotes Ibn Tulun directly: "I have greater need of the guard than you." Described as one hundred strong, these elite troops were of Ghur (central Afghani) origin, finely outfitted, and physically intimidating – they are said to have terrified the populace of al-Fustat.

The reminder of Abbasid-era reliance on military slaves and freedmen is useful. But the story has a different point: Ibn Tulun set principle aside for political gain. It was a delicate balance, but the *amir* was adept. Ibn al-Mudabbir drove home the point himself. On receiving the demand for his guard, Ibn al-Mudabbir replied: "There is something at work with this man – he turns down offers of gifts and cash, but then demands fighting men!" Ibn Tulun pressed his advantage: a further anecdote recounts another written exchange between the two men. Ibn Tulun, in a brief note, forced Ibn al-Mudabbir to acknowledge that, like Shuqayr, he had written letters to Iraq disparaging the new governor's approach to office. By now wary of Ibn Tulun's ambitions, the harried finance director promised to limit himself to public expressions of gratitude and support. This bought him only limited time.

The veracity of such stories cannot be checked. The snippets of direct speech, for example, are likely invented. But the essential ingredients seem reliable. A key source of information are financial documents (preserved on papyrus). They show that Ibn al-Mudabbir was head of the Egyptian fisc in this period and suggest that he was responsible for unpopular fiscal measures. More to the point is that Ibn Tulun, according to both Egyptian and Iraqi sources, convinced the caliphal administration to transfer the finance director from Egypt and give him control over its fiscal system. A first episode occurred around 868–869; Ibn Tulun forced Ibn al-Mudabbir from office and had him imprisoned in al-Fustat. He replaced him with a certain Muhammad ibn Hilal, a more pliable official. A cloth fragment bearing the Islamic date 256 (= 869–870) refers to Ibn Hilal and so constitutes useful, non-literary evidence of the shakeup.

But Ibn Tulun faced counter pressures, probably the influence of Ibn al-Mudabbir's Iraqi network. He reluctantly reinstated the finance chief, though without relenting pressure on him. Ibn al-Mudabbir, bowing to reality, finally requested transfer to Syria in 871–872. This is the likely point at which Ibn Tulun assumed formal control over Egypt's finance offices (Ar., *kharaj* and *ma'una*; the latter term is not always clear but appears to have been used both for some kind of fiscal office and a branch of the police services). It followed direct communication with the caliph in Samarra. The measure of his confrontation with Ibn al-Mudabbir can be taken on different levels. Each man, no doubt, was a stubborn actor, determined to have his way. Little surprise that matters turned vindictive: six years later, while on campaign in Syria, Ibn Tulun would turn on Ibn al-Mudabbir yet again, as will be described below.

But the confrontation went beyond the personal. The two men, working with powerful circles at the imperial center, pursued irreconcilable aims. Ibn Tulun was intent on redefining relations between Egypt and the Abbasid state. Ibn al-Mudabbir, for his part, hewed to the terms of his office: he was responsible for the supply of revenue and goods from the province to Iraq. Each man, in other words, relied on ties to the imperial center, but on quite different terms. But it should be stressed again that although Ibn Tulun was vying for supremacy in Egypt, he never severed relations with Samarra. This goes to the all-important role played by patronage – personal networks – in Abbasid imperial politics. This was a politics that the *amir* was now engaged in at the highest level. It might be described more generally in this way: Ibn Tulun was striking a difficult balance, asserting himself over Egypt while remaining reliant on his allies and the caliphate in Iraq.

Ibn Tulun's triumph over Ibn al-Mudabbir was a turning point. He now controlled the fiscal and political resources necessary to see through his growing ambitions. The confrontation took several years to play out. Concurrent events played their part as well though, admittedly, it is difficult to make sense of the order in which they took place. No less significant a turn in Ibn Tulun's fortunes had occurred a bit earlier, around 869–870, in the midst of the confrontation with Ibn al-Mudabbir.

These next events are a bit involved. In the midst of the confrontation with Shuqayr and Ibn al-Mudabbir, word reached Egypt of the execution of Bayakbak, the individual to whom Ibn Tulun owed his initial appointment. Bayakbak's violent death, carried out on orders from the caliph al-Muhtadi, was noted earlier. The latter figure, though known typically (and perhaps ironically) as the most pious of Samarra's caliphs, was clearly not above hard political decisions: al-Tabari, the Baghdadi historian, describes a grisly scene in which al-Muhtadi has Bayakbak's head tossed to a crowd of his own men. Little surprise that al-Muhtadi himself fell soon thereafter to the mayhem of Samarra.

The violent deaths of the two men – the Turkic commander and the pious caliph – marked, however, an important turn in bringing to a close the worst of the internecine violence at the imperial center. Most of the principal actors in the decade-long drama were by now either dead or exhausted. Al-Muhtadi's successor, al-Mu'tamid, the fifteenth Abbasid caliph, would reign for over twenty years (870–892), a period during which relative calm was restored to the Iraqi capital. Ibn Tulun and the new caliph would develop a close working relationship. It was born of shared antagonism toward al-Mu'tamid's overbearing sibling, the prince al-Muwaffaq. We turn to these developments shortly.

The point here is that al-Mu'tamid was also an ally of Bayakbak's successor, Yarjukh (d. 872). The same al-Muhtadi had transferred Bayakbak's offices to Yarjukh, including responsibility over Egypt, this on the heels of Bayakbak's execution. There is evidence that Yarjukh, another of the Turkic commanders of Samarra, was a party to the killing. As a military ally of the court, in other words, he had risen to prominence in the manner of many of his peers.

His appointment as vice-regent speaks to his connections in Abbasid court circles, but also to the standing arrangement by which Turkic commanders were continually assigned to al-Fustat. His appointment, in turn, marked another lucky step in Ibn Tulun's career. The sources speak of close ties between the two men. Al-Balawi describes them as considerably warmer than those with Bayakbak, referring to Yarjukh as "among Ahmad ibn Tulun's chief supporters." He cites, for example, their household connections: Yarjukh, at some unspecified date, had married Ibn Tulun to his daughter Khatun. She would bear Ibn Tulun's eldest son, al-Abbas. Here, again, is indication of Ibn Tulun's ambiguous relations with the Samarran military: while maintaining a studied distance from his fellow Turkic soldiers, he was careful to nurture contacts with given circles of these men.

On receiving his appointment, Yarjukh confirmed Ibn Tulun's assignment as resident governor. But he went a step further, thereby expanding the *amir*'s formal reach. He assigned him the districts centered on two cities, Alexandria – the famed Mediterranean port – and Barqa, also a coastal town, located to the west in historic Cyrenaica.

Ibn Tulun no doubt celebrated the gesture of confidence. The sources indicate that local officials in both Alexandria and Barqa were either removed or placed under the *amir*'s authority. Ibn Tulun also gained new ground against Ibn al-Mudabbir: the latter, temporarily in prison, is said to have been deeply unsettled by Yarjukh's decision. Ibn al-Mudabbir was reinstated, as previously noted, but, with support from Yarjukh, Ibn Tulun now held the stronger hand. Ibn al-Mudabbir put in for transfer to Syria shortly after Yarjukh's decision was announced. Of his three aims, Ibn Tulun had achieved the first, a commanding position over al-Fustat and the local imperial administration.

PACIFICATION AND THE TULUNID MILITARY

Ibn Tulun's new authority – his near full control over Egypt's fiscal offices – was tied closely to Yarjukh's decision to confirm him in office. It also coincided with the ascendance of the new caliph, al-Mu'tamid, with whom, as just noted, Ibn Tulun would soon enjoy working relations. Yarjukh himself soon disappeared; al-Tabari reports that he died in 872, his funeral attended by no less than the caliph himself, an indication of the commander's standing. By that point, however, Ibn Tulun was firmly situated in Egypt. He would repay his debt to Yarjukh, following the latter's death, by relocating the commander's family to Egypt, providing them with income and property.

Ibn Tulun owed his ascendance, however, to more than the support of the Samarran high command and Abbasid court. His political skills are also to be credited, be it an ability to exploit high-level relationships or, as it turned out, missteps by Shuqayr and Ibn al-Mudabbir. Al-Balawi insists on the point: Ibn Tulun's early success had very much to do with this instinct of making the most of opportunity. It went beyond favors granted by powerful supporters. Deeper political currents, and the *amir*'s ability to exploit them, played their part as well. We turn now to Ibn Tulun's second aim: the consolidation of control over Egypt.

Ibn Tulun assumed office at a point of surging instability across the Abbasid realm. The unrest took different forms. The Zanj uprising in southern Iraq, as noted earlier, was to preoccupy the Abbasid court throughout this period. But much of the upheaval involved spillover of the political violence in Samarra, particularly into Syria. There, local forces and imperial appointees – including Samarran military governors – fought for influence rendering Syria nearly unmanageable. In most cases, and in both direct and indirect manner, the unrest took the form of direct opposition to Abbasid authority. Smelling blood, local actors, including the Zanj leadership, challenged the empire in ways that in more settled times would have been ill-advised at best.

Developments in Egypt are a case in point. Ibn Tulun arrived in al-Fustat with central authority in question, both in the Nile Delta region and Upper Egypt. Long simmering tensions with Egypt's southern neighbors were now also on the rise. Ibn Tulun's mandate must certainly have included securing order across the province, the responsibility of any governor. And therein lay considerable potential rewards. If successful, Ibn Tulun was guaranteed greater access to the economic and human wealth of the Nile Valley. Success would offer, as well, closer relations with Egypt's military command and thus, in turn, a tighter grip over the province.

It took time but, by 875 or so, the forces at Ibn Tulun's disposal overcame a variety of local challengers. There are six episodes to account for in which Ibn Tulun took part. They are difficult to describe: the main actors are mostly obscure, and the sources provide few details about their grievances and scale of activity. There is also little information about who chose to follow these men, though all but one of the incidents was rural, so it seems likely to have been some combination of peasants, slaves, and tribesmen. It also appears that a combination of social, religious, and economic factors was at work; with the payment of ever-mounting taxes as a specific source of resentment. Discussion of the Egyptian economy in this period comes later. What follows here is an account of the events themselves.

Ibn Tulun played only a minor part in the first of the six episodes. Leading the imperial response to the rebels prior to Ibn Tulun's arrival was Yazid ibn Abdallah, his long-standing predecessor in al-Fustat. The uprising had played out mainly in the Nile Delta. Initiated early in 866 by an Arab tribal chief, Jabir ibn al-Walid al-Mudliji, and joined firstly by his tribesmen, it drew in a wider following, including elements of the Coptic Christian populace. Added to the mix was a prominent Alid figure, Ibn al-Arqat. It is difficult to account for the presence of the Alids at this point in Egypt's history, that is, their number, the reason for their presence in the province, and the extent of their local following. References in al-Kindi and al-Balawi point, however, to a discernible Alid presence in leading anti-imperial resistance, and Alid elements as bearing the brunt of repressive measures by the caliphate and its local officials.

By this point, the Turkic-Central Asian military dominated the local administration and thus led the way in responding to the rebels. The sources name, among the individuals holding top offices and leading units in the field, Buhm ibn al-Husayn, Tukhshi ibn Balbard and, notably, Azjur al-Turki. It is difficult to check each of the individual references (and be sure about the form of the individual names). But the impression of a near monopoly of authority by personnel of Turkic-Central Asian origin seems clear. Also clear is that Ibn Tulun could call on substantial and experienced military forces immediately on taking office. Azjur, possibly a member of a prominent free family of Turkish-Central Asian origin, headed the main police units (Ar., *shurta*) twice in 867–868 before assuming the office of governor for a brief period immediately before Ibn Tulun's arrival. His example is useful; it points to the likelihood that these officers acted collectively, that is, as a regime. Al-Kindi describes Azjur, for example, as making key decisions both in and out of office. His dating of events indicates, furthermore, that Yazid ibn Abdallah remained active in Egypt *following* the end of his tenure as governor, leaving the province only in 869, a full year after Ibn Tulun's arrival.

It is here, in al-Kindi's account, where Ibn Tulun makes his appearance, again, if only in a secondary role. The information, which is vague, concerns the final stage of the rebellion. The imperial forces, with reinforcements sent from Iraq, had worn down their opponents, often, it seems, with great violence. So, for example, late in the rebellion, Turkic-Central Asian units carried out a slaughter of Ibn al-Arqat's followers. Al-Kindi refers also to the sacking of local villages, and repeated acts of symbolic violence, for example, the display of severed heads. The leaders of the rebellion, including Ibn al-Arqat, finally surrendered. Ibn al-Arqat, after an attempt at escape, was dispatched to Iraq with a letter from Ibn Tulun presumably announcing the delivery of the prisoner and the victory itself. The indication, in other words, is that Ibn Tulun carried out the task early in his tenure.

The five other episodes of local resistance occurred with Ibn Tulun in charge. One dated to 867, the second to 869. An Alid – a claimant to descent from the Prophet Muhammad's household through his son-in-law and eventual successor, Ali ibn Abi Talib (d. 661) – is said to have instigated a revolt, about which the sources provide little detail: Ahmad ibn Muhammad ibn Tabataba is said to have appeared initially between Barqa and Alexandria before moving into Upper Egypt. Ibn Tulun sent a force against him under Buhm ibn al-Husayn. Buhm routed Ibn Tabataba's forces and returned to al-Fustat, the rebel's head in hand.

Leading the movement of 867 – the earlier of the two episodes – was Ibrahim ibn Muhammad, better known as Ibn al-Sufi. He was a more difficult opponent. Like Ibn Tabataba, Ibn al-Sufi claimed Alid descent. His base was in Upper Egypt, his forces responsible at one point for the sack of Asna, a large commercial town along the Nile. Ibn al-Sufi routed the first of the armies sent by Ibn Tulun, adding insult by torturing its commander, one Ibn Yazdad, then displaying his corpse in public. Ibn Tulun sent a second force led by Buhm. The latter succeeded in defeating Ibn al-Sufi near the town of Akhmim, killing many of his men, though without capturing the Alid leader himself. (Ibn al-Sufi was soon to reappear.) Al-Balawi describes Buhm's return to al-Fustat in useful detail. Ibn Tulun, in a public ceremony, presented the commander with an honorary robe, several fine horses and a belt of burnished gold.

Ibn Tulun then faced a third and more difficult opponent: Abu Abd al-Rahman al-Umari. Two accounts survive of al-Umari's movement: al-Balawi provides one, and al-Maqrizi, the dean of late medieval Egyptian historians, the other. Al-Balawi says nothing of al-Umari's background. He indicates only that al-Umari came to prominence when word spread of attacks on Muslims by the Beja, an indigenous, partially Christianized people resident along the Red Sea in Upper Egypt. Al-Umari is said to have become incensed on hearing of these assaults. He organized forces, attacked the Beja and, after defeating them, established a local presence, drawing on his success and pious standing.

At this point Ibn al-Sufi reappeared: his remaining forces clashed with those of al-Umari. Defeated, Ibn al-Sufi fled again, only to be chased by Tulunid forces under Buhm's command. Having reached Mecca, Ibn al-Sufi was arrested and sent to Ibn Tulun. The latter jailed him in al-Fustat, but only after displaying Ibn al-Sufi in a public ceremony, a ritual act of humiliation that Ibn Tulun would use against other opponents as well. (Ibn Tulun later released Ibn al-Sufi in what al-Balawi describes as an act of charity. The former rebel retired to Medina, where he later died.)

Al-Maqrizi's account of al-Umari's appearance is more substantial. It has al-Umari claim Medinese origin, specifically descent from the second of the Prophet's successors, Umar ibn al-Khattab (d. 644). He goes on to say that al-Umari arrived in al-Fustat – he provides no date – to study with prominent Muslim scholars. Following a brief sojourn with the Aghlabid court in Qayrawan (in modern-day Tunisia), he returned to Egypt, his scholarly bona fides in hand. He used these much as Ibn al-Sufi and Ibn Tabataba had done, though without the Alid ingredient: as a carefully shaped religious pedigree with which to bid for local authority. All three leaders appear to have found receptive audiences in newly Islamized districts of Egypt.

Al-Umari, according to al-Maqrizi, made his way specifically to Upper Egypt, after learning of the wealth produced by its gold and emerald mines. These mines had long played a key part in the economic history of Upper Egypt and the Red Sea. Al-Umari is reported to have assembled a labor force of slaves – most of Nubian background – with which he established an enclave in the region of Aswan. Al-Maqrizi speaks directly to al-Umari's scholarly reputation as a source of legitimation. His supporters, to whom he provided arms and horses, were almost certainly Arab tribesmen, many of whom were likely first-generation migrants to the area.

His presence disrupted a long-standing diplomatic and political balance in the area. It seems unsurprising that a response quickly emerged. To the south lay the Nubian kingdom of Maqurra. The Abbasids, having inherited from the Umayyads relations with various Christian polities in Nubia, had kept the frontier mostly quiet. They did so with a combination of diplomatic ties and commercial exchange, in which traffic in slaves and other goods figured prominently. Al-Umari's turn to slave labor and, especially, his apparent effort to cut in on gold production, seems like a reasonable explanation for the worried reaction. His fighters – if al-Maqrizi's reporting is sound – clashed repeatedly with forces dispatched from Maqurra and al-Fustat alike. Al-Umari proved stubborn, as his defeat of Ibn al-Sufi suggests. Al-Maqrizi indicates that the scholar-turned-local boss also exploited internal divisions in Maqurra by taking up with a disaffected claimant to the Nubian throne.

Al-Umari's activity ended abruptly, shortly after an apparent attempt to negotiate a settlement. He is reported to have claimed that he had no argument with Ibn Tulun: his aim, he stated, was to defend Islam against non-Muslim detractors, that is, local Nubian and Beja forces. It is implied that he and Ibn Tulun were natural allies. The bid for reconciliation collapsed, however, with al-Umari's assassination. His killers, two of his own freedmen, displayed his head to Ibn Tulun in a show of (transferred) loyalty. Ibn Tulun turned once again to public ceremony: he invited rural leaders to identify the head as that of al-Umari then turned angrily on the two assassins. He decried their action: "This was the last thing that either I or God would have seen happen." He had them executed and their bodies placed on public display. He then attended to the washing and burial of al-Umari's head in proper Muslim fashion.

Ibn Tulun's indignation was cynical, at least in part: the killing of al-Umari, after all, rid him of a serious political irritant. He was now free to turn his attention to two remaining challenges. There was, first of all, the activity of a certain Abu Ruh, described as a follower of Ibn al-Sufi, in the Delta region around Alexandria. The account, by al-Balawi, is useful on two counts. It points to the rural areas of Egypt as the main venue of unrest and offers key details on Ibn Tulun's relations with his military command.

Abu Ruh, according to al-Balawi, was a son of the Egyptian countryside (Ar., *rif*) and, by virtue of his upbringing, knew its roadways
well. Turning to banditry, he cut off local byways and disrupted traffic. (Al-Balawi does not say as much, but it is easy to imagine the
effect on local agrarian markets and central revenue collection.) Ibn
Tulun responded with a force led by one Yalbaq al-Tarsusi. The latter,
al-Balawi tells us, had served with Ibn Tulun on the northern Syrian
frontier. Abu Ruh routed these units, forcing Ibn Tulun to devise new
tactics. He sent one force, under Ibn Jayghawayh, to cut off access
between al-Fayyum – the area of Abu Ruh's main activity – and the
other oases to the south and west, and a second force under Shu'ba ibn
Kharkam. It fell to Shu'ba to attack Abu Ruh head on. He did so, wip-
ing out the rebel's forces and forcing Abu Ruh's surrender. Ibn Tulun
promptly executed two of the latter's supporters and, as was current
custom, exhibited their bodies.

The final challenge arose in Barqa, a city located in Tripolitania,
the province immediately east of Egypt. Yarjukh, as noted earlier, had assigned the city to Ibn Tulun in 870. A brief reference in
al-Balawi's *Sira* indicates that it was a walled city and, as a likely hub
of Mediterranean commerce, probably a source of significant revenue. The Arabic sources say only that the local populace rose against
Muhammad ibn al-Faraj al-Farghani, the Abbasid governor. They
expelled him from the city and secured its gates. Ibn Tulun responded
with considerable force. He is said to have sent at least two armies
with a small fleet and siege equipment. Leading one army was Lu'lu',
an up-and-coming member of Ibn Tulun's inner circle.

Ibn Tulun instructed his commanders to exercise restraint. The
effort to reach a settlement failed, however, when the rebels attacked
Tulunid forces, killing Ibn Tulun's lead commander. Lu'lu', taking
charge, counter-attacked successfully. Ibn Tulun rewarded Lu'lu' with
a noisy public reception, a ceremony much like that staged for Buhm
ibn al-Husayn earlier on. The victory, if the Egyptian sources are to
be trusted, settled the question of Ibn Tulun's authority. Al-Balawi
reports that the Egyptian people now viewed Ibn Tulun – and, perhaps, by extension, the Turkic-Central Asian regime in Egypt – with a
mix of newfound respect and dread.

THE IMPERIAL STAGE

Ibn al-Sufi's appearance dates to around 866–867; the triumph over the rebels in Barqa to 875: Ibn Tulun's consolidation of authority over Egypt spanned roughly ten years. The various episodes were, at one level, local events rooted in the instability of the Egyptian country-side, and, especially, the deep hostility generated by the heavy hand of imperial tax collectors. But they were connected as well with the upheaval sweeping the empire. Notable, in this sense, was the promi-nent role of Alid leaders and their followers, although, as in the case of al-Umari, opposition to central authority took other forms as well. It was a variety of religious and political opposition confronting a fragile, uncertain Abbasid center.

In subduing his local opponents, Ibn Tulun thus secured the second of his overarching goals, a tighter hand on Egypt. Given his success, and Egypt's standing as a major province, it seems hardly surpris-ing to see Ibn Tulun take on a wider regional role. His third abiding aim – redefining relations with the Abbasid house – comes into focus here. These threads were closely bound: Ibn Tulun's consolidation of authority translated, in large measure, into a necessary reshaping of his ties to the imperial center. The focus in this chapter is on the events themselves; we will discuss the full significance of Ibn Tulun's relations with his Abbasid overlords later.

To track these relations, it is useful to turn the clock back several years. Two developments, in particular, informed Ibn Tulun's approach to the Abbasid center. The first occurred in Syria. It involved the con-tentious activity of Isa ibn al-Shaykh al-Shaybani (d. 883). Ibn al-Shaykh, scion of a notable Arab family and, at this point, governor of southern Syria, had come to prominence under Bugha the Younger (d. 868), a Samarran Turkic commander. He had done so in leading imperial units against local rebels, initially in Azerbaijan then in Syria itself. Appointed governor of Palestine in 865, he elected, in 866, to delay recognition of the newly ascendant caliph al-Mu`tazz. The decision was perhaps dictated by Bugha the Younger's poor relations with the new ruler, a further sign of the political divisions in Samarra. Ibn al-Shaykh was forced briefly from office, but then reappointed, this time to Palestine and Jordan.

It is at this moment that his career collided with that of Ibn Tulun. The year was 869–870, the same year in which Yarjukh, as vice-regent of Egypt, confirmed Ibn Tulun's appointment to office, and al-Mu'-tamid ascended the throne. Ibn al-Shaykh, keenly aware of the troubles facing the Abbasids in Samarra, made a bid for autonomous rule. He allied himself with local Arab forces and laid claim to Damascus. Driven presumably by the need to raise support and cover his military costs, he seized the annual tribute dispatched from Egypt to Iraq by Ibn al-Mudabbir (then still in office in al-Fustat). The amount is reported as 750,000 dinars. Ibn al-Shaykh is also reported to have refused the oath of loyalty to the newly appointed al-Mu'tamid.

The new caliph sent envoys to convince Ibn al-Shaykh to surrender the funds. On Ibn al-Shaykh's refusal, the caliph turned to Ibn Tulun, ordering the governor to march on Damascus, and directing Ibn al-Mudabbir to provide the *amir* with the necessary funds. Ibn Tulun promptly established, according to the biographers, a new army of African ("black") and Byzantine ("Rum") slave troops and ordered up the requisite supplies and equipment. Appointing his brother, Musa ibn Tulun, to represent him in Egypt, Ibn Tulun then marched north toward the Sinai. But events took an unexpected turn: word came of the arrival in Syria of an imperial force under one Amajur al-Turki (d. 877), a caliphal freedman and another of the Samarran commanders. Amajur ousted Ibn al-Shaykh and assumed the governorate of southern Syria.

Ibn Tulun thus had little option but to abort the campaign and return to al-Fustat. The biographers say nothing of his reaction; it is impossible to know whether Ibn Tulun considered a challenge to Amajur. The sources do indicate that Amajur was wary of Ibn Tulun from the start. He is said to have written to the caliphal court, sometime shortly after taking office, to warn of Ibn Tulun's emerging strength. Al-Mu'tamid responded by ordering Ibn Tulun to appear in Samarra for reappointment. Ibn Tulun, sensing a ruse, is said to have sent a personal representative instead. It was an early step in a complex dance of relations between Ibn Tulun and the Abbasid center.

Ibn Tulun had also to contend with the needs of his new army. Al-Balawi indicates that the pressure on Ibn Tulun was not simply to house and feed the new units. He also refers to a rise in social tensions: the residents of al-Fustat complained that there was little room in the principal mosque and, presumably, the town proper, for the new troops. (One is reminded of the tensions in Baghdad decades earlier that led al-Mu'tasim to found Samarra.) Ibn Tulun responded with the construction of a new administrative and military center. He named it al-Qata'i' (literally, "the consignments") (see Map 3). The construction and population resettlement seem to have moved quickly; al-Qata'i' soon replaced al-Fustat as Egypt's administrative and military center. It also earned a nickname, al-Maydan ("the square"), after the immense plaza that Ibn Tulun had built alongside a new palace. Sometime later, Ibn Tulun broke ground as well for the new congregational mosque and, in an area adjoining the new settlement, a new hospital.

Ibn Tulun's campaign against Ibn al-Shaykh, in sum, ended nearly as soon as it began. A reasonable guess is that the Abbasid decision to turn to Amajur – the latter would govern southern Syria for eight years – was taken in response to Ibn Tulun's ambitions. It was noted earlier that Ibn al-Mudabbir and Shuqayr had already warned of Ibn Tulun's aims: imperial observers were likely wary of the Egyptian governor and his mounting authority. So, his detractors in Samarra overruled the decision to let him deal with the Syrian rebel, opting instead to send Amajur from Iraq.

The controversy surrounding Ibn al-Shaykh's activity, however, was eclipsed by the Zanj revolt, described earlier, a development of far greater consequence. It was in this context that Ibn Tulun's relations with the Abbasid center took on a sharper edge. The confrontation turned on his determination to control Egypt's revenue. At issue initially were the mounting costs of fighting the Zanj. Ibn Tulun's chief antagonist – as seen already – was Abu Ahmad al-Muwaffaq, the caliph's older brother. The Abbasid prince was a veteran of Samarra's bitter history. His father, the caliph al-Mutawakkil, had fallen to Turkic assassins in 861; al-Tabari's detailed account places the young Abu Ahmad on the scene, an eyewitness to the act of regicide. He subsequently led Samarran units against Baghdad, this during a round of Iraqi civil war in 865–866. The outcome, in part, were close ties to elements of the Turkic-Central Asian command and, specifically,

Musa ibn Bugha (d. 878), a prominent figure in Samarran military and political circles. A falling-out with al-Muhtadi in 870 then led al-Muwaffaq to withdraw to Mecca in self-imposed exile. It was upon the accession of his brother, al-Mu'tamid, that he returned to Iraq and full political activity.

The new caliph – a political novice – no doubt turned to his brother for much needed advice and support. He assigned him initially to provinces of northern Iraq, probably in an effort to strengthen the frontier with Byzantium. Three years later, in 874, he designated him second in line to the throne after his own son, al-Mufawwad. It is at this point, probably, that Abu Ahmad earned the regnal title of al-Muwaffaq. His chief responsibility, however, was the Zanj campaign. It was here that his return to public life grew controversial.

It was not a question of al-Muwaffaq's abilities, as he would eventually oversee the Abbasid triumph over the southern Iraqi rebels. The problem lay in his appetite for decision-making: he moved quickly to exploit his military connections and greater political experience to lord it over his younger sibling. He effectively claimed the role of regent, caliph in all but title. His overbearing style played out in his treatment of al-Mu'tamid but also in his angry relations with Ibn Tulun. These tensions were born, in part, of disagreement over Ibn Tulun's uneven effort in offsetting the costs of the Zanj campaign. Al-Muwaffaq, at first it seems, viewed it as a refusal to support imperial aims. But the rivalry, as ego-driven political battles so often do, turned personal. Each man was determined to have his way, whether in guiding the caliph and his court, or in asserting himself on the wider imperial stage. A confrontation was inevitable.

THE LAST YEARS IN OFFICE
877–884

Ibn Tulun had achieved much in his first decade in office. The years that followed would see him lead two military campaigns deep into Syria and the frontier; further consolidate authority over Egypt; and engage in a dramatic showdown with rivals in Iraq led by al-Muwaffaq. Fortune turned, however, with significant setbacks, both in Egypt and on the Byzantine frontier, and the onset of the *amir*'s final illness.

For context, it would be helpful to review conditions in the later ninth-century Abbasid Empire. The imperial state was in crisis: warlords and commanders – military men with a taste for politics (and a chip on their shoulders) – had asserted different levels of autonomous rule in a variety of provinces. They typically did so with the support of local political and social elites. Political risk-taking was rife, in Egypt but also Khurasan, the Caucasus, and North Africa, where the Aghlabid house would hold sway into the early tenth century. The imperial center – the caliph, his court and ministers, and the military brass in Samarra – had too few resources on hand to respond effectively. Military and political options were constrained by civil tensions in Iraq and the demands of the Zanj revolt. And, in many cases, local Muslim elites no longer felt beholden to the empire as they once did. Abbasid claims to pre-eminence over the Islamic realm were no longer binding either on powerful local actors or regional populations.

Imperial disintegration, however, was gradual and uneven. The Abbasid state retained a potent presence, especially in urban centers. The chaos of the Samarra period peaked with the assassination of the caliph al-Muhtadi in 870 and a round of civil violence during which, among other developments, the Samarran rank and file rose against their superiors. The accession of al-Mu'tamid in that same year, and al-Muwaffaq's return from exile, brought needed respite to the battered capital. A return to order appears to have had much to do with al-Muwaffaq's ties to the Samarran military and, in particular, Musa ibn Bugha. The latter, a veteran commander, had survived the chaos and, now, emboldened by ties to the Abbasid court, held sway over much of the imperial army. The shift largely ended overt intervention by the military command in the affairs of state.

But the calm was relative: relations between the caliph and al-Muwaffaq turned bitter. The common view is that al-Mu'tamid acquiesced early in his reign to al-Muwaffaq's aggressive style, preferring to devote his time to drink and the favors of courtesans. But this moves too quickly over the evidence. It seems clear that the young ruler, less capable than his brother, seldom enjoyed the upper hand. But, at several turns, he stood his ground. The sibling confrontation cannot have done much for the standing of the caliphate. It fed the sense of crisis at the Abbasid court, and led to an uneasy alliance between Ibn Tulun and al-Mu'tamid. The two men, after all, shared an interest in blunting al-Muwaffaq's edge.

The relationship, and al-Muwaffaq's refusal to see it develop, was connected initially with the Zanj war. The conflict was having a corrosive effect on the stability and legitimation of the empire; its considerable costs had mounted. Al-Muwaffaq, charged with crushing the rebels, sought out every source of fiscal, political and military support. Such was the context for his angry relations with Ibn Tulun. Frustrated with the slow pace of the campaign, al-Muwaffaq accelerated his demands for revenue from across the empire. The sources report that Ibn Tulun, unlike other governors, refused to comply, at least not in the manner demanded of him by his rival. Al-Muwaffaq's impatience with his headstrong counterpart seems hardly surprising.

Al-Muwaffaq's ability to maneuver was partly shaped by decisions on al-Mu'tamid's part. Over a four-year period (871–875), the caliph slowly expanded his brother's formal authority, appointing him, for example, over provinces in Syria and Iraq. This culminated with a grand ceremony in 874 in which al-Mu'tamid announced the administrative division of the empire. He assigned the western provinces, including Egypt, to his son and principal heir, al-Mufawwad, and the eastern provinces to al-Muwaffaq. The ceremony is not easy to interpret. The caliph presumably had a smooth succession in mind: his son and brother were designated as heirs apparent. But it seems also to have been an effort to strengthen his own hand, at least in the sense of maintaining a check on his brother: he could assign, or so he hoped, but also strip away.

If this was the young caliph's aim, it fell short. For al-Muwaffaq, the new arrangements offered an official, and thus welcome, claim to authority. The wrinkle, however, concerned Egypt. Could he make legitimate claims on its revenue? It would seem not as the province was assigned formally to al-Mufawwad. Al-Muwaffaq appears not to have cared: the demands of the Zanj campaign trumped the niceties of the succession agreement. The Abbasid regent, paying lip service to the new scheme but little more, pressed ahead with his demands on Egypt and thus his quarrel with Ibn Tulun.

The confrontation of regent and governor played out initially in an exchange of heated correspondence. Al-Muwaffaq, in a first letter, acknowledged that he could not request funds that were properly the claim of al-Mufawwad. But, insisting that Ibn Tulun was duty bound to serve the demands of the empire, al-Muwaffaq dispatched an envoy, Nihrir, to secure badly needed funds. The caliph, recognizing a further opportunity to frustrate his brother, warned Ibn Tulun of Nihrir's intent to sow dissension in al-Qata'i'; Nihrir, he warned, was al-Muwaffaq's spy. Ibn Tulun placed Nihrir under house arrest before returning him to Samarra with, it should be said, a considerable payment to be delivered to al-Muwaffaq. This was no act of deference. Al-Balawi indicates that Ibn Tulun simultaneously initiated close relations with al-Mu'tamid. The end result was an agreement to begin secret payments to the harried monarch. The account specifies four annual payments sent by Ibn Tulun between 875 and 879.

For Ibn Tulun it was a matter of winning new political ground. The considerable wealth at his disposal, Egypt's revenue, was his instrument. He had made the one payment to al-Muwaffaq probably in 875.

It did little to satisfy the restless regent; al-Muwaffaq, in a further letter, complained that the payment fell short. Ibn Tulun, writing back,
and in measured fashion, pointed to al-Mu`tamid's succession plan. He
had only to answer to al-Mufawwad, to whom the caliph had assigned
Egypt, and was under no obligation to al-Muwaffaq. Ibn Tulun went
further: he accused his rival of violating the terms of the succession
arrangement and seeking to replace him as the duly appointed governor of Egypt. The accusation was abuse of office. Ibn Tulun added
that his own advisors were pushing him to drop al-Muwaffaq's name
from the Friday prayers, pressure he could ignore for only so long. He
closed, in less subtle manner, with a reference to the strength of his
own military, should al-Muwaffaq consider the option of force.

Al-Muwaffaq had enough. In early 876, he contacted Amajur, the
long-time governor of southern Syria, offering him Egypt in exchange
for a successful campaign against Ibn Tulun. Amajur, wary of the latter's strengths, begged off. Al-Muwaffaq turned next to Musa ibn
Bugha, his long-time ally. Ibn Bugha duly organized an army and set
off from Samarra. The campaign caused a stir in Egypt. Reacting to a
stream of intelligence reports, Ibn Tulun ordered defensive measures
taken in Egypt, including a new fortress on the Nile island of Rawda
and new construction at the port in Alexandria.

Better news followed. Ibn Bugha's troops – Turkic and Central
Asian units from Samarra – protested delays in the payment of their salaries and refused to proceed. The campaign collapsed, Ibn Bugha having reached no further than al-Raqqa, a town on the upper Euphrates.
This is yet another indication that divisions within the Samarran military were far from mended. It may also be that the Samarran rank
and file was leery of marching as far as Egypt against an opponent of
unknown strength.

The campaign was Ibn Bugha's last: the commander died early in
877 shortly after his return from al-Raqqa. His death allows for a brief
reflection on the trajectory of Ibn Tulun's career. Ibn Bugha's father,
Bugha the Elder (d. 862), had been seized, with his sons, in the province of Khurasan in 820. He thus entered Abbasid imperial service at
roughly the same moment as Tulun (Ibn Tulun's father) and, it seems,
on similar terms, as a captive offered military service. Bugha proved

his loyalties, leading, over a long career, major campaigns in support of Abbasid rule. One campaign, in 844–845, was against nomadic raiders in central Arabia in an effort to protect pilgrimage routes to the Hijaz. A second campaign took him into Armenia, a difficult province for the Abbasids, between 850 and 855.

The son, Musa, picked up where his father left off. His first name and other references suggest that he and his father were converts to Islam. Unlike his father, however, he participated actively in imperial political life (Bugha, either by choice or necessity, remained mostly outside the imperial center, playing only a passing role in the turmoil in Samarra itself). In this sense, Musa ibn Bugha's career mirrored that of Ibn Tulun. The offspring of Abbasid freedmen and the eldest sons of Samarra's military households, each man was a child of empire. And each man developed a taste for public life: each knew to exploit the frailty of the Samarran regime to advance personal and political interests.

Ibn Bugha's disappearance was Ibn Tulun's gain. And fate smiled twice: news of Ibn Bugha's failure was followed by the announcement of the death of Amajur, the Syrian strongman. Al-Balawi, using the Arabic term *iqbal* or "good fortune," describes the turn of events as yet further sign of Ibn Tulun's abiding luck. The governor responded promptly, organizing his forces for a new campaign north into Syria. Unlike on the first occasion – the scrubbed effort against Ibn al-Shaykh in 870 – Ibn Tulun moved across the Sinai and into Syria without hindrance.

THE NEW SYRIAN CAMPAIGN

This next campaign needs further context. Concerns facing the Samarran court included the Zanj revolt as well as turmoil on the Abbasid-Byzantine frontier. New activity by Byzantine forces in the late 870s intersected with upheaval on the Abbasid side of the frontier in the far north of Syria. Sima al-Tawil, the governor of Tarsus, had attacked his counterpart in Antioch and taken the city. At this point, al-Muwaffaq was still in charge of the frontier districts; seeking to replace Sima, he appointed a certain Urkhuz ibn Ulugh Tarkhan. The latter exacerbated matters by seizing revenue raised by the people of Tarsus for the mercenary garrison at Lu'lu' (Loulan), an outlying fortress. The garrison, hungry and disgusted, responded by surrendering the fortress to the Byzantines. Self-serving activity on the part of local Abbasid commanders – reflecting long-time divisions in Samarra's military – thus undercut imperial defenses and frustrated al-Muwaffaq's efforts at securing central control over the frontier districts.

This provided an opening to al-Mu'tamid: he announced the assignment of the frontier districts to Ibn Tulun. The references to his decision are patchy. Al-Balawi reports that Ibn Tulun had first asked al-Muwaffaq to assign him the frontier; the regent, as seen earlier, had formal authority over the now troubled region, so the request was appropriate. Al-Muwaffaq turned him down. The caliph's announcement followed shortly thereafter. Given al-Muwaffaq's writ, on what grounds did the caliph act? The answer, in part, may be that the caliph was motivated to act by al-Muwaffaq's failure to properly administer the frontier districts or, at least, find the right people to do so. But the crisis offered the caliph opportunity to gain ground against his brother. This is to see provincial appointments as informed by the sibling rivalry, each of the two Abbasid brothers using them to maneuver against the other.

As for Ibn Tulun, the appointment meant two things: it enhanced his political standing while strengthening his hand against al-Muwaffaq. Consumed by the Zanj campaign, the Abbasid regent had little choice but to acquiesce. The caliphal appointment, in 876–877, occurred as Ibn Tulun was firming his hold in Egypt itself. In selecting a resident governor to represent him in Tarsus, Ibn Tulun turned first to his brother, Musa ibn Tulun. When he refused, Ibn Tulun dispatched a long-time client and loyal commander, Tukhshi ibn Balbard. The choice was a happy one: Tukhshi is said to have carried out his duties well, with wide local support, up to his death in 882. Al-Balawi also refers to a truce (Ar., *hudna*) reached between Ibn Tulun and the Byzantine monarch; Ibn Tulun charged Tukhshi with seeing to its enforcement in Tarsus.

It was at this point that word came of Amajur's death in Damascus. The announcement was timely. Amajur had taken office in Syria eight years earlier, and is reported to have been an effective governor, successful in bringing order to a contentious province. There is indirect evidence of his ties to the Syrian religious establishment. It consists of a large and elegant Qur'an in several volumes. Known appropriately as "the Qur'an of Amajur," it was originally housed in a mosque in Tyre, the southern Lebanese port city. Over time the volumes were broken up, its precious pages scattered across private and state collections (some pages are today on display in prominent museums). A formulaic statement containing Amajur's name, inscribed on every second page of the work, bespeaks his role as the project's patron and, by extension, his appeal to Islamic values in the public arena.

It was an opportune time, in Ibn Tulun's view, to intervene in Syria. Al-Balawi has Ibn Tulun derive considerable relief from the death of Amajur and, in Iraq, Musa ibn Bugha. He immediately ordered preparations for the new campaign. To represent him in Egypt in his absence, he appointed his son and heir, al-Abbas, and tapped al-Wasiti, his long-time advisor, to serve as regent. It was an acknowledgment of al-Abbas' lack of experience (the significance of which will become clear shortly).

To prepare the way, Ibn Tulun contacted Ali ibn Amajur, the deceased governor's heir. The latter, an adolescent, was supported by his father's inner circle, led by one Ahmad ibn Da'bash (or, possibly, Dughyash). The names of both men suggest that, like Ibn Tulun himself, they were second-generation members of the Samarran military. The indication, in turn, is that Ibn Tulun had previous contact with Ibn Da'bash. The *amir*, in his letter, demanded supplies and fodder for his forces. Ibn Amajur offered no resistance, acting no doubt on the advice of his father's companions.

The Tulunid army entered southern Palestine near al-Ramla. Ibn Tulun was received, with great deference, by Muhammad ibn Rafi, Amajur's lieutenant. Al-Balawi describes the scene: "Ibn Rafi, on sighting Ibn Tulun, immediately dismounted, approached the *amir*, and kissed his hand." It is a passing reference and cannot be checked. But one reading is that Ibn Rafi met the governor not as a representative of the Abbasid state but as a power broker in his own right. Ibn Tulun, in response, retained Ibn Rafi in office as his deputy. Ibn Tulun rode on to Damascus, Syria's chief city. On hand was Ibn Da'bash and

others of Amajur's circle; they saw to the formal announcement of Ibn
Tulun's name from the city's mosques. As he had done with Ibn Rafi,
Ibn Tulun formalized ties with Ibn Da'bash. Al-Kindi, the Egyptian
historian, indicates that Ibn Tulun remained in Damascus long enough
to be "assured of conditions therein." Al-Kindi does not elaborate nor
is it clear how long Ibn Tulun remained in the city. The point is that
Ibn Tulun sought to make his presence felt before resuming his way
north. Relations with Ibn Da'bash, his men and, perhaps, the local
Muslim religious establishment: these were the makings of a political
network in Syria's largest city.

Homs came next. Ibn Tulun initially retained Amajur's man, one Isa
al-Karkhi, as local chief. A veteran of the fighting in Samarra, he had
become, however, a controversial figure. Al-Balawi indicates that Ibn
Tulun, on hearing complaints from the local populace, replaced al-Karkhi
with Ayman al-Turki. Al-Tabari reports things differently: Ibn Tulun
made the appointment after locals assassinated al-Karkhi.

It is unfortunate that the sources say so little about these individuals – Ibn Amajur, Ibn Da'bash, Ibn Rafi, and the other members of
Amajur's circle. Again, most were probably Samarran military men
by origin. They were Ibn Tulun's contemporaries and may well have
known each other for years. For the local urban population, on the
other hand, these men were unwelcome intruders. This was true, in
any case, of those acting as freebooters, unrestrained by either local
customs or imperial authority (Amajur and Ibn Balbard were, it seems,
exceptions). Efforts at local resistance, such as al-Karkhi's killing, can
thus be explained. These dynamics worked to Ibn Tulun's advantage in
the short term, but it is easy to suppose that, for many inhabitants of the
Syrian towns, the governor was but a new iteration of a persistent woe.

This is speculation, however, as the sources also offer few details
on Ibn Tulun's administration of Syria or the campaign itself. A fourteenth-century Christian text, known as the *Continuatio*, refers to incidents in Palestine: it speaks of pillaging and wanton destruction visited
by Ibn Tulun's forces, especially his African troops, on the local populace. Given that no other source offers such information, it is difficult
to assess the value of the description. The Arabic sources only speak of
the key events of the campaign.

Ibn Tulun moved on from Homs, having encountered few obstacles to this point. A difficult challenge then arose in Antioch, Ibn Tulun's last stop before the frontier. The town had fallen to Sima al-Tawil, also a controversial figure, as seen earlier. Al-Balawi describes him as a renegade, and has Sima's relations with the local populace grow sour: "He interacted badly with the populace of Antioch, and they had come to detest him." Ibn Tulun, on reaching the city, worked initially to convince Sima to surrender the city without issue. He sent envoys to arrange a face-to-face meeting. The two men spoke at length, in both Turkish and Arabic, a further hint of long-standing relations between Ibn Tulun and his Samarran peers. Sima proved stubborn, however, and the siege that followed ended with his murder. Al-Balawi has locals, anxious to bring the fighting to an end, secrete Ibn Tulun and his men into the Antioch fortress. Further violence was averted with Sima's assassination, not by Tulunid troops – Ibn Tulun had ordered his counterpart to be taken alive – but by members of the city's populace. Tulunid forces proceeded to plunder Sima's treasury, livestock, and supplies. The city in hand, Ibn Tulun moved north to the Byzantine frontier.

To this point, one thinks, Ibn Tulun was satisfied with the course of events. Matters took a turn, however, once the Tulunid force entered Tarsus. Relations between the city's inhabitants and the Abbasid center had grown uneasy, as suggested earlier, and the arrival of the new army in 877–878 did little to resolve things. Al-Balawi puts it this way:

> [Ibn Tulun] entered Tarsus with a large army and great show of strength. Prices were badly affected, and the city's streets grew crowded with his officers and troops. The populace grew furious; tensions rose between the locals and Ibn Tulun's men. Town leaders finally sought him out, in the typical rough manner of the people of the frontier, forgetting that it was in the face of a daunting foe [likely a reference to the Byzantine army] that they confronted him. They addressed him: "Our territory – may God preserve the *amir* – is overrun by your men and, because of you, our livelihood is threatened, our markets in turmoil. Either remain with a smaller force that our town can support or depart."

Ibn Tulun chose to withdraw, but only following a tense exchange with his commanders, who pressed him to continue the fight against the Byzantines. Ibn Tulun countered with a wobbly argument: he wished to fool the Byzantine forces into thinking that if he, with his large army, could not hold the city, then they too would have little success in doing so.

How to read the passage? It is the case that Basil I (r. 867–886), the Byzantine monarch, now on campaign along the frontier, was pressuring Abbasid defenses. In this sense, the idea that further division within the city would play into Byzantine hands seems right. But al-Balawi, in his close account, seems more concerned with Ibn Tulun's personal connection to Tarsus. His view seems to be that the hostile reaction in Tarsus was both a personal and political setback for Ibn Tulun. The suggestion is that it did little for Ibn Tulun's reputation and seems to have strained relations with his own forces.

The setback in Tarsus notwithstanding, Ibn Tulun had accomplished much: entire districts of Palestine, Syria, and the Jazira were now under his nominal control. Ibn Tulun took measures to consolidate his presence in each province. Al-Balawi, always ready to play up the *amir*'s better qualities, sees behind each measure Ibn Tulun's "shrewdness and acuity of intellect," and a determination to prevent the newly seized regions from falling into a "disordered state." These are rhetorical flourishes best taken with a grain of salt. But this point is clear: Ibn Tulun had made a bid for authority over these central provinces and thus forced his way to the center of the imperial stage.

The appointment of local governors was a necessary step. Ibn Tulun turned to his military command: he kept Tukhshi ibn Balbard in Tarsus, appointed Ahmad ibn Jayghawayh over Harran, and Lu'lu', his long-time client, over al-Raqqa. It appears, shortly thereafter, that he assigned Lu'lu' overall command of the Syrian provinces. Al-Balawi adds that each commander in turn appointed his own men at the local level. The appointments came with the minting of new coinage on which Ibn Tulun attached his name to that of al-Mu'tamid. Specifically, Ibn Tulun affixed his name beneath that of the caliph and, on the obverse side, that of al-Mufawwad, the heir apparent. It was a show of loyalty, to caliph and heir apparent alike, but also a reminder of his own presence, using coins, one of the most effective social media of the time. Ibn Tulun had them minted in at least four locations: al-Rafiqa, from 878, Homs, from 879, Palestine, from 880, and Damascus, from 882.

*A Tulunid gold dinar, minted in Egypt in 883–884. One side of the coin features
the names of the caliph, al-Muʿtamid, and, below it, Ahmad ibn Tulun. The name of
al-Mufawwad, the heir apparent, appears on the reverse side.*

There exist few other details regarding Tulunid administration of
Syria and the Jazira. It is thus difficult to know how the appointments
worked out. It is important to note that the Tulunid presence was short
lived: Ibn Tulun would live only another six years, and Khumarawayh,
his successor, would struggle to sustain authority over these territories. It is probably correct to think that local populations viewed the
turnover to Tulunid control – if that is an apt characterization – as but
a new phase of imperial occupation. But the sources say almost nothing of either the conduct of the Tulunid governors or their relations
with locals. It does appear, as will be seen, that Ibn Tulun was chiefly
interested in his standing in Damascus, though he would also persist in
his commitment to Tarsus.

FATHER AND SON

As things turned out, Ibn Tulun had little time to concern himself
with Syria. Unexpected news arrived: al-Abbas, back in Egypt, had
turned against his father. Ibn Tulun prepared to return to Egypt. It
was at this point that he assigned the districts of Syria and the Jazira
to his lieutenants (Lu'lu' and Ahmad ibn Jayghawayh). He also took

the opportunity to settle scores with Ibn al-Mudabbir, who was then serving in Damascus. He had the former finance director arrested and seized his wealth, a practice of extortion known as *musadara*. Ibn al-Mudabbir, according to various sources, died in prison, presumably in Syria, in 884.

But Ibn Tulun's main worry was his son. The events of al-Abbas's action can be briefly described. Ibn Tulun had appointed al-Abbas over Egypt with al-Wasiti acting as regent. The latter soon faced a crisis as, according to the two biographies, al-Abbas fell under the influence of close companions. Among them were military men, said to have been jealous of Ibn Tulun's success and bent on taking advantage of the governor's problems on the frontier. More influential still was a small circle of Tulunid officials, local scholars and literati; the sources describe them as al-Abbas's inner circle. Their number included Ja'far ibn Hudhar, a poet and well-placed scribe.

These men, suspicious of Ibn Tulun, had pressed al-Abbas to act. They turned first against al-Wasiti. Al-Balawi reports that he had kept Ibn Tulun informed of his son's erratic performance; his letters, however, had been monitored by Mahbub ibn Raja, a rival, who provided copies to al-Abbas. Knowing too well his father's likely reaction to news of dissent in Egypt, al-Abbas panicked. He ordered local markets stripped of goods and supplies, and his father's treasury emptied. He also pressured local merchants for loans. The supplies and monies allowed him to raise an army and, it seems, buy the support of military commanders. He also ordered the arrest of al-Wasiti and Ayman al-Aswad, another of his father's advisors.

Al-Abbas, the two senior Tulunid advisors in tow, headed north to Alexandria then west into Ifriqiya. Ibn Tulun arrived in Egypt shortly thereafter. A side note: it was shortly after his return that the governor oversaw the completion of the new mosque in al-Qata'i'. The structure, as noted in the introduction, was not simply a fine example of ninth-century Islamic architecture but also a significant statement of authority on Ibn Tulun's part. It appears that construction was complete by Ramadan 879, so, again, just as plans were made for the campaign against al-Abbas. Ibn Tulun would make much ceremonial use of the mosque. It seems right to think that he was motivated, in part, by the need to repair the political damage inflicted by his son.

Back in al-Qata'i`, Ibn Tulun checked first on the condition of his treasury. On learning of the sums seized by al-Abbas – al-Balawi gives a figure of two million dinars – he summoned his finance director, Ibn Ukht al-Wazir. The latter, facing the governor's wrath, pleaded that al-Abbas had left him little option but to submit. Ibn Tulun forgave the hapless official and turned to organizing a response to his wayward offspring, now on the march along the North African coast. Thanks to increasingly desperate letters sent by al-Wasiti – one wonders how the latter managed to smuggle them out – Ibn Tulun was able to track his son's progress.

He opted first for negotiation, sending a delegation of four men: Ma'mar al-Jawhari, a wealthy merchant and long-time associate; the two ranking members of the judiciary, Bakkar ibn Qutayba and al-Sabuni; and Ziyad al-Ma'dani, a freedman described as an effective mediator. The meeting with al-Abbas culminated in an emotional appeal by al-Ma'dani that reduced the participants to tears. The delegation then withdrew, convinced of their success: the Tulunid prince was sure to return home under their supervision.

Al-Balawi tells the story well. He quotes a letter sent by Ibn Tulun in which the *amir* invited his son to submit but included the warning that he would strike hard if al-Abbas refused. But Ibn Hudhar, the scribe and poet, convinced al-Abbas that his father – Ibn Tulun – could not be trusted. The delegation returned the next day, again, certain that al-Ma'dani had won the day. Al-Abbas pressed Bakkar, the elderly and respected judge, for his opinion. Bakkar's response was measured: "Your father promised not to turn against you, but your decision to believe him is between you and God." Al-Abbas's allies heard enough: they forced the Tulunid prince to send the delegation home and press on with the campaign.

A confrontation with the Aghlabids soon followed. The family, of mixed Arab and eastern Iranian origins, had been appointed to Ifriqiya in the early part of the ninth century and, like the Tulunids, had maintained relations with the Abbasid house. Their long dynastic presence in Ifriqiya, however, had led to a far greater degree of autonomy than that asserted by Ibn Tulun. Al-Abbas's appearance was certainly unexpected, as was his aggressive conduct. The Tulunid prince, whether on his own accord or pressed by his advisors, had evidently decided on the ouster of Ibrahim ibn Ahmad (r. 850–902), the ninth of the Aghlabid line. This may be, however, how later writers, including al-Balawi, chose to understand the campaign: the indications are that al-Abbas acted very much in ad hoc fashion. It is difficult to know for certain what he had in mind.

The revolt – if that is a suitable term – reached a low point early in 879 at the town of Labda. Al-Abbas ordered his troops to sack the Aghlabid city, this despite (or, perhaps, because of) the willingness of its local governor to negotiate a surrender. Al-Abbas went on to engage a small Aghlabid force before suffering a rout outside Tripoli at the hands of larger Aghlabid units backed by forces dispatched by Ilyas ibn Mansur al-Nafusi. The latter served as a provincial governor of the Rustamids, an Ibadi Muslim dynasty and significant North African power, located further to the west. Al-Abbas, outnumbered, abandoned his troops and supplies and fled back to Egypt.

The sad adventure collapsed. Al-Wasiti, having escaped, briefed Ibn Tulun on the sorry state of his son's forces. Having prepared to march on his son, Ibn Tulun now opted for a smaller elite force led by a certain Tabarji (we only have the one name). The Tulunid force swept away what remained of al-Abbas's units. Upon their return to al-Fustat, al-Abbas in hand, Tabarji and his officers were greeted with an elaborate welcome, much like that held for Buhm and other commanders on previous occasions. Ibn Tulun then saw to the punishment of al-Abbas. He ordered the construction of an execution site complete with a raised area (from which Ibn Tulun would preside), a short ceremonial road, and an elaborate platform. As the governor and, presumably, numerous troops and civilians looked on, al-Abbas, outfitted in handsome robes and a new turban, was ordered to flog his main supporters. Ibn Tulun then ordered his son to dismember Ibn Hudhar; the latter's remains were tossed from the platform to the dusty ground below. Ibn Tulun then placed his son under house arrest.

The grisly ceremony is but further suggestion of Ibn Tulun's taste for political showmanship. As for the so-called revolt, al-Balawi treats it as a hapless affair. Al-Balawi's portrayal of al-Abbas, which he likely drew directly from Ibn al-Daya, is scathing. The latter author, as an illustration of al-Abbas's character, describes how he once ordered the live burial of three attendants for little more than whispering out of earshot. Al-Balawi, for his part, comments on al-Abbas's unstable character and offers further examples. Other sources follow suit. Al-Maqrizi, the later historian, includes a grim anecdote in which al-Abbas murders the infant son of a favorite concubine. Reports of the revolt itself appear to have spread quickly; it is likely to have been closely monitored across the empire. If, for Ibn Tulun's control over Egypt, a dangerous moment, for his detractors it must certainly have been welcome news. It also presented Ibn Tulun with something of a diplomatic mess, drawing him into tense contact with neighbors to the west, the Aghlabids and, in a more limited sense, the Rustamids. Given the extent of the crisis, it is striking that Ibn Tulun opted to spare his son further punishment.

The full impact is hard to measure. Al-Balawi does not mince his words: "al-Abbas's affair ... set in motion the decline of Ibn Tulun's well-laid plans." But this seems misleading. Ibn Tulun returned to full authority over Egypt and, indeed, used the opportunity of the crisis to further consolidate his hold over the Nile Valley. Among other steps, he replaced al-Abbas with his second son, Khumarawayh, as heir apparent. Ibn Tulun also remained central to Syrian politics, with commanders in charge of major cities. That he weathered the revolt can also be seen in his decision to organize a new campaign into Syria. The campaign took place in 882–883. Its culmination serves as a reminder of how quickly political fortunes can turn, even for the most audacious of actors.

TARSUS AND DAMASCUS

The sources provide little information on the period immediately following al-Abbas's action. It was brief in any case: new developments drew Ibn Tulun back into Syria and the melee of high imperial politics. The sequence of events is hard to pin down. Egyptian sources

– al-Kindi and al-Balawi – offer different chronologies. Where they agree (mostly) is on the events themselves, and the manner in which the storm of activity was connected to the confrontation with al-Muwaffaq and Ibn Tulun's determination to have a hand in imperial decision making. Al-Tabari, the Baghdadi historian, offers useful information as well, although his dating is also problematic.

This last period of Ibn Tulun's career turned on four developments. Each will be considered in turn, as will the manner in which each event overlapped with the next. The developments were as follows: the defection of Lu'lu', Ibn Tulun's man in Syria; an attempted flight by the caliph, al-Mu`tamid, to Egypt; a confrontation in Mecca, this on the occasion of the Hajj; and new turmoil in Tarsus. Ibn Tulun clearly had a great deal on his plate. If one event precipitated the decision to march back into Syria, it was likely the betrayal of Lu'lu'. This is, in any case, how the biographers put it.

Lu'lu' was Ibn Tulun's principal agent in Syria. He had become a significant member of the Tulunid household at an early point. Nothing is said of his background, although he is identified as a eunuch (Ar., *khadim*), and the single name, Arabic for "pearl," signifies that he was of slave origin, though, at this stage, he is likely to have been a freedman. His role in crushing the revolt in Barqa years earlier has been noted already. It seems, from that point forward, that Ibn Tulun entrusted his client with wide ranging responsibilities, especially in military matters. The decision to assign him Syria is one such indication. A further reference by al-Tabari indicates that the forces under Lu'lu''s command were considerable, further indication of his place in the Tulunid hierarchy. The reference is significant: Lu'lu', according to the reference, was stationed in al-Raqqa, a former Abbasid center in northern Iraq, and thus within striking distance of the imperial heartland. There is nothing in the sources to indicate that Ibn Tulun had plans to march on Samarra. But the reference suggests that he was prepared for such an option.

Word that Lu'lu' had defected, therefore, must have struck hard. The sources speak of clashes between Lu'lu' and others of Ibn Tulun's officers around 881–882 in northern Syria. Lu'lu' then contacted al-Muwaffaq, offering his forces and treasury (the revenue that he otherwise would have turned over to Ibn Tulun). The Abbasid regent, deep in the fight against the Zanj, hurried to accept. Al-Tabari indicates that Lu'lu', upon his arrival in Samarra, took immediately to the field. His long account of what were the final stages of the war makes clear that the Tulunid units played a key part in landing the final blows against the Zanj. The year was 883–884. Al-Tabari has a rider from Lu'lu''s army deliver the head of Ali ibn Muhammad, the Zanj leader, to al-Muwaffaq.

The reasons for Lu'lu''s defection are unclear. There was the activity of Muhammad ibn Sulayman, a high-ranking Abbasid official and, more particularly, Lu'lu''s close advisor. Ibn Sulayman is reported to have had a falling-out with Ibn Tulun, and one view is that he convinced Lu'lu' to switch loyalties. There may be something to the suggestion; Ibn Sulayman would later command the Abbasid forces that destroyed the Tulunid state in 905, so relations between Ibn Tulun and Lu'lu''s circle were clearly strained. But this remains guesswork: the sources, unfortunately, offer too little guidance as to Lu'lu''s thinking. Ibn Tulun reacted, in any case, with the new campaign into Syria. The decision to confront his former client sparked a new round of antagonism between the governor and al-Muwaffaq. The antagonism would play out in three locations and, as one might expect, the renewed confrontation only further destabilized the empire.

It is important to add that Lu'lu''s defection constituted a further rift in elite Tulunid circles, coming as it did on the heels of al-Abbas's clumsy bid for power. In preparing to depart al-Qata'i' for the new foray into Syria, Ibn Tulun appointed Khumarawayh as his deputy over Egypt. All indications are that Abu al-Jaysh – Khumarawayh's nickname – served his father loyally; there is no evidence to the contrary. But the sources point out that Ibn Tulun took al-Abbas with him. The half-brothers were hardly allies and, indeed, the opposite was probably true. But Ibn Tulun was taking no chances: he removed al-Abbas from Egypt as guarantee that his irksome son would have no opportunity to cause further trouble.

Ibn Tulun approached Lu'lu' much as he had Sima in Antioch and, thereafter, al-Abbas. He first sent letters containing a mix of conciliatory language and threat. Lu'lu' ignored the gesture, which stands to reason. The situation was new and Ibn Tulun's options more limited. In the case of Sima and al-Abbas, the governor had been ready with military force and, in both cases, acted on that option. In the case of Lu'lu', however, that was a difficult choice. Lu'lu', for one thing, commanded a Tulunid army: was Ibn Tulun prepared to challenge him in battle? And armed confrontation would have obliged Ibn Tulun to march from Syria into Iraq, the imperial heartland, meaning perhaps a direct clash with the caliphate.

It bears repeating that Ibn Tulun never challenged the Abbasid state itself directly: he was committed to its survival. An armed confrontation with al-Muwaffaq, however, may have been a consideration. But, as things turned out, Ibn Tulun was quickly distracted from his plans for Lu'lu'. Again, our sources disagree on sequence. What appears is that Ibn Tulun – either before reaching Damascus or shortly after his arrival – was pressed to deal with two other crises. These events were all linked to the persistent divisions of Samarran political and military life, and especially the rift between Ibn Tulun and al-Muwaffaq.

There was, first of all, a new crisis in Tarsus, where Tukhshi ibn Balbard had remained as Ibn Tulun's deputy. He, in turn, shortly before his death, probably in 883, had appointed Khalaf al-Farghani as his successor. Khalaf is briefly identified as a client of the Tulunid family. Ibn Tulun, for unstated reasons, ordered Khalaf to arrest a certain Yazman. Things get a bit complicated here. The sources say nothing of why Yazman, another of the Samarran military men, was in Tarsus. Possibly a eunuch (like Lu'lu', he is tagged as a *khadim*), he had previously served al-Fath ibn Khaqan who, in turn, had been a close associate of al-Mutawakkil, the first of the Samarran caliphs to fall to Turkish conspirators. (Al-Fath was assassinated alongside the caliph in 861, some twenty years previous, which suggests the extent to which tensions endured in the Abbasid capital.) Yazman's arrest may well have been tied to the rivalry with al-Muwaffaq: the latter was al-Mutawakkil's son and had been an eyewitness to his father's killing. This is to see Yazman, in other words, as having remained in al-Muwaffaq's circle.

Violence followed on news of the arrest: Yazman's supporters turned on Khalaf, forcing him from Tarsus and placing their man in charge. Again, this was probably more than a local squabble: Ibn Tulun and al-Muwaffaq often used proxies against one another. Al-Tabari reports that Yazman's backers saw to the ritual cursing of Ibn Tulun at the Friday prayers. This was to be the first of two such incidents; the second was to occur later that same year on al-Muwaffaq's behest. Al-Balawi, for his part, has Ibn Tulun later send a letter to Yazman in which he raged against his opposition to Khalaf (his client). He then prepared to march on Tarsus.

Ibn Tulun faced, however, a third and more serious crisis. Either on his way to the frontier or in the midst of mobilizing his army in Damascus, Ibn Tulun received word that al-Mu`tamid – the beleaguered caliph – had left Samarra for Syria and Ibn Tulun's protection. It was a first step, as the sources indicate, in a plan to transfer the seat of the caliphate to Egypt. Al-Mu`tamid had used a hunting expedition as his excuse to escape the Iraqi capital with a small entourage of Abbasid courtiers. Further news followed: no sooner had al-Muwaffaq learned of the caliph's escape than he convinced key allies to arrest al-Mu`tamid and his entourage and return them to Iraq. He then placed the caliph, his younger brother, under house arrest in Samarra.

As a remarkable turn of events, it needs a bit of background. Al-Balawi indicates that Ibn Tulun had been in correspondence with al-Mu`tamid prior to his departure from Egypt. Ibn Tulun had pressed the Abbasid ruler to make for Egypt where he could exercise his proper authority free of al-Muwaffaq's meddling. The invitation was controversial, both in Iraq and Egypt. Al-Balawi describes an encounter at which, on the advice of al-Wasiti, Ibn Tulun sought out a prominent religious scholar, Muhammad ibn Isma`il ibn Ammar, one of Ibn Tulun's many political prisoners. Ibn Ammar advised Ibn Tulun to drop the idea. He argued that the caliph's presence in al-Qata'i` would overshadow the governor's authority. Ibn Tulun rejected the advice, however, and ordered Ibn Ammar returned to his cell.

Al-Balawi, always quick to praise Ibn Tulun, wants us to believe that the governor acted dutifully: he had sworn the oath of loyalty (Ar., bay`a) to the caliph and thus felt responsible for his protection. The explanation ought not to be dismissed out of hand. But nor should it be forgotten that Ibn Tulun had much to gain in his confrontation with al-Muwaffaq had the plan succeeded. Instead, al-Muwaffaq, offering lavish payments to two allies, Sa'id ibn Makhlad, a leading Abbasid courtier, and Ishaq ibn Kundaj, the military governor of Mosul, managed to thwart what would have been a profound embarrassment. The two men hurried to al-Haditha, a village to the west of Samarra, where they arrested the caliph.

Ibn Tulun reacted by calling for an assembly of tribal notables, legal scholars, and senior judges at the principal mosque in Damascus. He summoned these men from Egypt, Syria, the frontier districts with Byzantium, and northern Iraq, all provinces under his ostensible authority. At the head of the Egyptian delegation, ten individuals in all, was Bakkar ibn Qutayba, the chief *qadi* (judge). It was a remarkable moment. Though only one of numerous public events organized by Ibn Tulun, it was certainly the most ambitious. If, on other occasions, however, the governor sought advice, or so he claimed, this time he insisted on ringing endorsement. Michael Bonner, a modern scholar, has studied the Damascus Assembly in detail. The following comments draw on his discussion.

Seizing on al-Muwaffaq's decision to have al-Mu'tamid arrested, Ibn Tulun commissioned a document of censure. He ordered ten copies drawn up, which he sent to his provincial agents, to be read aloud (and, presumably, posted) in the principal mosques of larger cities. The original documents have not survived but the early Egyptian historians, al-Kindi and al-Balawi, include versions of the text in their respective accounts. It was for the arguments laid out in the document, of course, that Ibn Tulun sought unambiguous expressions of support. But the public reading, and the elite gathering itself, were significant gestures in their own right. The entire performance – this is the main point – constituted an enormous gamble. Ibn Tulun was dictating terms not simply to the imperial house, in the person of al-Muwaffaq and his circle, but the imperial religious establishment as well.

Ibn Tulun was blunt in protesting the treatment of the caliph. The claim was that al-Muwaffaq, in an illicit bid for supremacy, had violated the terms of the sacred oath by which Muslims pledged their fealty to the caliph, the "viceregent" (Ar., *khalifa*) of God. The treatment of al-Mu'tamid thus violated the obligations that defined family, kinship, and patronage, the very stuff that sustained Islamic communal unity. For this, Ibn Tulun insisted, al-Muwaffaq had forfeited his relations not only with the caliph and all Muslims, but with God himself. If the community, and its religious leadership, therefore, were to regain proper standing in the eyes of God, then it was only appropriate for al-Muwaffaq to be stripped of office. Ibn Tulun, strikingly, then raised the stakes: he called on Muslims to take up arms against the Abbasid regent. It was a call for *jihad*. This last step, as Bonner points out, was an obvious stretch. *Jihad* against the Byzantines or, say, nomadic forces on the Central Asian frontier, was one thing. A declaration of religious war against a member of the Abbasid house was quite another.

The gamble fell short. For a brief and dramatic moment, Ibn Tulun managed to command wide public attention. The sources tell us that most of the assembled notables voiced support for the censure document. But Ibn Tulun cannot have been satisfied. For one thing, he failed to secure the backing of Bakkar ibn Qutayba. The latter, as head of Egypt's judiciary, exerted considerable legal and moral influence; Ibn Tulun very much wanted his support. But Bakkar proved ambivalent: he agreed to condemn al-Muwaffaq but held back from throwing the full weight of his opinion behind the regent's deposition. His position is hard to make out, but it appears that he adopted a narrow, legalistic definition of al-Muwaffaq's "sin." It was a far narrower position, in other words, than Ibn Tulun demanded. Quick as ever to punish, Ibn Tulun ordered Bakkar's arrest and imprisonment.

Al-Muwaffaq wasted no time in responding. He ordered a written rebuttal drawn up and had the imams of leading mosques ritually curse Ibn Tulun in their Friday sermons. Al-Balawi quotes much of the rebuttal document, and we can rely on Bonner's translation for a flavor of the exchange. It should be noted, as well, that both documents – Ibn Tulun's censure and al-Muwaffaq's reply – were written as if issued by al-Mu'tamid though the caliph likely played little part in the proceedings. (He was under house arrest, and thus, presumably, silenced, a political turn that few observers can have missed.) Al-Muwaffaq's document reads in part:

> Now the enemy of God, who has deviated from the community of the Muslims, the man known as Ahmad ibn Tulun, has openly committed acts of rebellion and heresy everywhere … he has renounced the true

religion and has opposed the [caliph]. Accordingly, when [the caliph] ascertained the truth of the matter, and knew of his disbelief, he dissociated himself from [Ibn Tulun] before Almighty God and ordered that he be cursed.

In confronting one another, Ibn Tulun and al-Muwaffaq knew to use verse as well. This was expected: poets had long served in the Near East, as they continue to do today, as political instruments. Al-Kindi, in his chronicle, provides long excerpts by contemporary poets, writing both in support of Ibn Tulun and on behalf of his detractors, chiefly al-Muwaffaq. Not a great deal is known of the poets that wrote for Ibn Tulun: they appear to have been local Egyptian writers employed by the Tulunid court. Al-Muwaffaq, on the other hand, could draw on the voices of more prominent writers.

Muhammad ibn Da'ud ibn al-Jarrah (d. 908) was among the harshest of Ibn Tulun's critics. A member of a prominent secretarial family, with close ties to al-Mutawakkil and, it seems, al-Muwaffaq himself, Ibn Da'ud had savaged Ibn Tulun in verse on previous occasions. So, for example, in a biting piece, preserved by al-Kindi, Ibn Da'ud had mocked Ibn Tulun for cowardice and tyranny following Musa ibn Bugha's failed campaign in 877. Following the Damascus Assembly, and Ibn Tulun's defeat at Tarsus (see below), Ibn Da'ud spoke out again. In a new poem, undated, he seems to comment on both events, charging Ibn Tulun, once again, with a mix of cowardice and oppression, this time against the people of Tarsus.

His example only underscores the intensity and highly public nature of Ibn Tulun's fight with al-Muwaffaq. It is difficult to know how far the rivalry might have gone: Ibn Tulun had soon to turn his attention again to Tarsus, and, in any case, would be dead within the year. There are, unfortunately, only hints as to what each man was thinking. Al-Muwaffaq, for his part, was immersed in the fight against the Zanj, although, thanks in good part to the arrival of Lu'lu' and his troops, triumph lay close at hand. But he was distracted, and, militarily speaking, one wonders if he was prepared for another confrontation. What of Ibn Tulun? There is evidence that he considered a military option. It concerns the size and quality of the army that Ibn Tulun assigned to Lu'lu' at al-Raqqa, from where an attack against al-Muwaffaq might plausibly have been organized. Another indication is that shortly after Ibn Tulun's death, Tulunid forces clashed with units led by Ishaq ibn Kundaj in northern Syria. Ibn Kundaj, as we have seen, was an ally of al-Muwaffaq and one of two men delegated to arrest al-Mu'tamid at al-Haditha.

And there is the fighting that occurred at Mecca in 883–884, on the eve of Ibn Tulun's death. These events, obscure, are thus hard to explain. Al-Balawi reports that Ibn Tulun had directed Khumarawayh, as his father's deputy in Egypt, to send a small force to the holy city. Its orders were to suppress all public mention of al-Muwaffaq's name. The occasion was the Hajj, a perfect opportunity to score political points (for Ibn Tulun and al-Muwaffaq alike). But an alliance of Iraqi troops sent by al-Muwaffaq and Meccan locals scattered the Tulunid units. A furious Ibn Tulun ordered the imprisonment of their commander, Ibn al-Sarraj, upon the latter's return to al-Qata'i'. Is the sequence of clashes an indication that Ibn Tulun was ready to march directly on his Abbasid rival? It remains unclear.

There remains one further event to consider: Ibn Tulun's march against Yazman in Tarsus. This was, it will be recalled, the second time that he led forces to the frontier. The earlier occasion, in 877–878, had concluded with Ibn Tulun's decision to withdraw following a tense confrontation with the local populace (unhappy over the presence of the large Tulunid force). Tensions between Ibn Tulun and the same populace proved more palpable still in this new episode.

The short campaign probably occurred immediately on the heels of the Damascus Assembly. Ibn Tulun marched north, first to al-Massisa, a southern Anatolian town near Tarsus. Sending envoys, as was his habit, he offered Yazman a guarantee of safe passage in exchange for a declaration of loyalty. Yazman chose instead to prepare the city for an extended siege: on arriving at Tarsus, Ibn Tulun found the city well defended, ballistae in place along its walls. The attack commenced in the midst of intense cold and driving rain. At some point, perhaps under pressure from the city's inhabitants, Yazman ordered a breach of waterworks holding back the Baradan River, which ran through the city. The ensuing flood swept across Ibn Tulun's encampment, forcing the governor and his troops to flee to the nearby town of Adana, their equipment and supplies ruined.

THE QUESTION OF LEGACY

Ibn Tulun's good fortune had run dry. In al-Massisa, he is said to have
fallen ill after drinking spoiled buffalo milk. Suffering dysentery and
vomiting, he grew so weak as to be unable to ride. Taken initially
to Damascus, he was transported by litter and boat to al-Qata'i`. He
died, to use the Islamic dating, on the 10th day of Dhu al-Qa`da, 270
(May 5th, 884).

Al-Balawi's long account of these final weeks refers to Ibn Tulun's
arrival in al-Qata'i`; his repeated angry encounters with medical pro-
viders; his final collapse; and the public mourning that followed. His
informants describe the governor as a difficult patient, rejecting the
advice of his medical team for the misguided and, ultimately, fatal care
provided by a household favorite. Al-Balawi dwells on these details,
partly to entertain his readers. But his account includes more serious
content: he speaks at length of the careful measures that Ibn Tulun
adopted to assure the transfer of power to Khumarawayh, his son and
successor.

The governor, first of all, ordered new steps against prominent
opponents. He had Lu'lu''s properties in Egypt confiscated, his
dependants sold to slave traders. (Lu'lu' himself was soon to fall from
favor, despite the defeat of the Zanj. Following his arrest by al-Muwaffaq and subsequent departure from Samarra, for reasons that are
unclear, Lu'lu' died in disgrace.) Ibn Tulun turned on other critics as
well, stripping them of their property and jailing them in al-Mutbaq,
the notorious prison in al-Fustat. The men included Mahbub ibn Raja,
a long-time Tulunid official, accused of having supported al-Abbas in
878–879; a certain Harthama, for having publicly spoken against the
legitimacy of the Abbasid caliphate; and Ziyad al-Ma`dani, for having
mocked Ibn Tulun's own claims to authority.

But Ibn Tulun also worked to reconcile with three individuals with
whom he had been at odds. For unstated reasons, he ordered Mahbub
ibn Raja set free and his property returned. Ibn Tulun also reached
out to Bakkar, the former chief judge, now in prison, punished for
his conduct at the Damascus Assembly. Bakkar rejected the overture
and remained voluntarily in his cell. His final comment to Ibn Tulun's

messenger, Nasim, a well-placed member of the Tulunid household, was that God would have the final say in determining the justice of his treatment. Ibn Tulun wept on hearing the response. (Al-Balawi reports that Khumarawayh had Bakkar released following Ibn Tulun's death. The elderly jurist died shortly thereafter.) And there was al-Abbas, to whom Ibn Tulun reached out with the offer of an honorary robe and an assignment to govern Syria. The gesture is puzzling given the many headaches that his eldest son had caused him. It is less surprising, however, if one considers the care with which Ibn Tulun approached his family members. On making the offer, Ibn Tulun spoke to al-Abbas at length on the virtues of supporting Khumarawayh. It was an offer of redemption, but came to nothing: assassins, sent probably by Khumarawayh, murdered al-Abbas shortly after their father's death.

If we follow al-Balawi, these measures combined firm-handedness and a turn to mercy, each a quality of far-reaching and enlightened leadership. No less a measure was the decision to advance the armed forces a full-year's salary. Al-Balawi provides much detail, throughout the *Sira*, on Ibn Tulun's efforts to create a formidable local military. It was the keystone of the Tulunid state, and the payment of salaries speaks to that aim. As al-Balawi is careful to note, Ibn Tulun ordered the payment to coincide with the oath of loyalty that the army was to take upon Khumarawayh's swearing-in. "It was with this moment in mind," the *Sira* has him say, "that I have gathered such wealth. The troops will rest easy knowing that whoever led them to war and grew their numbers would compensate them generously – only this way will we win over their hearts and minds!"

The payment of salaries occurred alongside yet a further step on Ibn Tulun's part: the declaration of his last will and testament to Khumarawayh himself. It was the last of the governor's grand ceremonies. It followed a private meeting with al-Wasiti, the *amir*'s long-time companion, in which he praised the latter's service and friendship. Well he might: al-Balawi, again quoting Nasim, a key informant, reports that al-Wasiti later broke from the Tulunids, offering his services to the new caliph, al-Mu'tadid (r. 892–902), in a confrontation shortly after Khumarawayh's rise to office. It occurred after

Ibn Tulun's death but counted nonetheless as a further defection by a leading member of Ibn Tulun's inner circle.

The ceremony for Khumarawayh was held before a gathering of military, religious, and civilian notables. In attendance were al-Wasiti, as the leading civilian member of the court, and Tabarji, a prominent field commander. The governor urged the assembled command-ers (Ar., *quwwad*) and household guardsmen (Ar., *ghilman*) to unite behind his son and insisted that they set aside their differences (the precise nature of which is left unstated). Their individual fortunes, and thus the future of the realm, were only assured by common effort. Ibn Tulun also noted efforts by his opponents in Iraq to undermine all that he had carefully put in place: they were to refuse the inducements offered them by al-Muwaffaq and his agents.

Ibn Tulun then addressed Khumarawayh directly. He spoke first of the annual tribute to be paid to the caliph, specifying al-Mu`tamid by name and citing an annual sum of 100,000 dinars. There was, he said, no duty more sacred: the revenue was to be delivered promptly and without fail. To do otherwise was to violate the terms by which the Tulunid house had sworn the oath of loyalty, the *bay`a*. Ibn Tulun, with this statement, declared his commitment to the Abbasid realm and, by implication, his refusal to support al-Muwaffaq.

But Ibn Tulun was also speaking to his legacy in reminding his audi-ence of his main achievement. Ibn al-Daya and al-Balawi refer often to the governor's success in managing the Egyptian economy. To make the point, al-Balawi details the wealth of Ibn Tulun's treasury and how he, the governor, expected Khumarawayh to use it properly. The numbers are impressive. Speaking to his son, Ibn Tulun underscored the need to manage these resources judiciously. He was to devote "the treasure of your realm" in tending to the needs of not only his military but the people of Egypt as well. The populace, Ibn Tulun insisted, would count on his generosity, much as they had done under Ibn Tulun himself. But it was a matter of careful management: "Every extravagance leads to ruin and collapse." He added that Khumarawayh was also to ignore the counsel of those seeking harm to the regime and its realm; Ibn Tulun, perhaps more than anyone, was keenly aware of the pressures, military and political, that would come to bear on his heir.

The governor closed the assembly with a call for God's blessing and guidance. The palace, al-Balawi tells us, shook from the force of the weeping that ensued. Ibn Tulun, exhausted from the effort, was carried off in a litter. But he remained vigilant to the end. The biographers include a brief episode in which Ibn Tulun insisted on inspecting the walls of al-Qata'i` a final time. Spotting several openings in the walls, he ordered these sealed. The symbolism is clear: the realm was now properly secured against its opponents.

Ibn Tulun died in proper Muslim fashion, his face turned to Mecca, the *shahada* on his lips. Al-Balawi refers to the enormous processions that accompanied the body to its burial site: a display of grief on the part of all Egyptians – Muslims, Christians, and Jews, free persons, clients, and slaves. The sources do not specify where Ibn Tulun was laid to rest. A single reference – to a small tomb (Ar., *turba*) located near Bab al-Qarafa, later one of the Fatimid gates of Cairo – comes from a later Egyptian scholar, Abu al-Hasan al-Sakhawi (d. 1497).

The expressions of general lament and grief were not confined to Egypt. Al-Mu`tamid is reported to have broken down on hearing the news. And the sources speak even of al-Muwaffaq's remorse: he is quoted as speaking eloquently of Ibn Tulun's commitment not only to the caliphate but to virtuous rule itself. Was the response surprising? The two men – Ibn Tulun and al-Muwaffaq – had after all been as two roosters in a common barnyard. The Abbasid regent may well have reacted with remorse, but another reading is to see the reports of his reaction as making the point that even al-Muwaffaq could not but acknowledge the caliber of Ibn Tulun's leadership.

3

GOVERNING EGYPT

In what manner did Ibn Tulun rule Egypt? As the new appointee, he was initially charged with two formal duties: presiding over the Friday prayer (Ar., *salat*) and assuring the flow of tax revenue (Ar., *kharaj*). The first element had to do with authority: a key moment was the pronouncement each Friday of the names of the caliph, the latter's heir-appointees, *and* the governor. It was an acknowledgment of legitimacy, thus an important public act. Ibn Tulun's reliance on symbol, ritual, and ceremony is a main topic of Chapter 4. The second duty concerned taxes and thus the administration of Egypt, the topic of this chapter.

The Arabic sources have Ibn Tulun govern Egypt with skill. They might be taken at their word: there are clear indications that the Tulunid economy flourished. But how to read these indications? What do they tell us of Ibn Tulun's approach to governance? The province had long been subject to imperial Arab-Islamic rule, under the Umayyad caliphate (661–750), then the Abbasid house following its rise to power in 750. Ibn Tulun followed the most able of his predecessors in governing Egypt with a firm hand but he also broke new ground. How so, and for what reasons? Our discussion begins with the written sources and, specifically, the works of Ibn al-Daya and al-Balawi. Their value as sources of information is clear, but they are to be read carefully for reasons considered below. The chapter then returns briefly to Ibn Tulun's appointment to Egypt. Our main topic, however, is Ibn Tulun's performance in office.

REPRESENTING IBN TULUN

Information on Ibn Tulun's two biographers is fragmentary, and neither author reveals much of himself directly. Ibn al-Daya and al-Balawi
were Muslim scholars, and both men were residents of tenth-century
Egypt. It was pointed out earlier that Ibn al-Daya, like his father,
worked in the Tulunid administration. He and his father, Yusuf ibn
Ibrahim, were also landholders. Drawing on his social network, Ibn
al-Daya cites well-placed members of Ibn Tulun's household; they
acted as his informants and it seems he listened closely. He likely produced his book late in the Tulunid period or shortly after the ouster of
the Tulunids in 905. Al-Balawi, for his part, probably completed his
book some decades thereafter. He too may have had access to surviving
members of the regime. He was trained as a religious scholar, probably in the Twelver Shi'i tradition. Brief biographical notices indicate
that he was a second-tier specialist in Prophetic teachings (Hadith).
His keen interest in Egyptian affairs seems obvious: his book, like that
of Ibn al-Daya, contains a wealth of useful detail.

Al-Balawi, writing after Ibn al-Daya, hoped to profit from writing the *Sira*. He opens with what reads like a response to a potential
benefactor without, however, identifying that person or providing
the latter's comment directly. He indicates that his patron expressed
disappointment with Ibn al-Daya's book. Al-Balawi expresses agreement: Ibn al-Daya failed to produce a clear and properly organized
account of Ibn Tulun's career. He promises to produce the sort of
book that he – the ostensible patron – expected. The statement seems
mean-spirited, given that al-Balawi owed much of his material to his
older colleague's work. The *Sira*, in large part, is an expanded version
of Ibn al-Daya's book. This is, at any rate, one reasonable description:
it bears repeating that no original version of Ibn al-Daya's text exists,
so it is difficult to know exactly how the two books compare.

On the basis of this small amount of information, and what is
known about Abbasid-era scholarly life in general, it is fair to see each
writer's writing as shaped by a pair of concerns. The first concern
was material: each man probably earned at least a partial livelihood
from writing and teaching. This was true of al-Balawi; Ibn al-Daya

perhaps earned his main income from his official duties and landed revenue. The second concern was moral: both men likely took their faith seriously. It would follow that each man took a deep interest in the fortunes and future of the Islamic realm. Such concern included close consideration of authority: what constituted sound leadership in Muslim society?

This question stands behind each author's representation of Ibn Tulun as a public figure. Four elements of their description stand out. First, Ibn Tulun governed in autocratic fashion: his was the final say in nearly every area of decision-making. Second, Tulunid governance was thus highly centralized: Ibn Tulun was not simply the final arbiter, but also held sway over all public offices, with the exception of the judiciary. Third, the governor relied heavily on a program of rhetoric and ceremony, in which a display of commitment to religion – the Islamic tradition – stood front and center. And, finally, Ibn Tulun relied no less heavily on repression. Was it a question of injustice? The theme, justice, will be addressed in due course.

The biographies rely heavily on short narratives (Ar., *akhbar*, sing. *khabar*), although, in some cases, they knit together a set of these "reports" into a single, longer "story," as in the account of al-Abbas's turn against his father. Such use of *akhbar* is typical of much Arabic writing of the early and medieval Islamic periods. Consider the following example: the story of Umm Uqba's petition to Ibn Tulun. It concerns, in part, the *barid*, the bureau responsible for intelligence gathering and the post. The story occurs in both biographies; the following is al-Balawi's more detailed version:

Abu Kamil Shuja ibn Aslam, the chamberlain (Ar., *hajib*), recounted the following: "Umm Uqba al-Arabiyya came one day to Ahmad ibn Tulun with her son Uqba. Ibn Tulun held her in high regard, taking special pleasure in her eloquence and rhetorical gifts; he welcomed her at every opportunity. She asked him to provide her son with a reputable job. Ibn Tulun said to Ibn Muhajir, who was on hand, 'See that her son is given honest work that will reflect well upon him.' Ibn Muhajir, director of the *barid*, appointed the young man to a district office and assigned him a monthly salary of ten *dinars*." Ibn Muhajir went on: "I was with Ahmad ibn Tulun three days later when Umm Uqba reappeared. She

said: 'I am grateful to the *amir*, God bless him, but furious with this
man.' She pointed at me. He said to her: 'But why?' She replied: 'He
was to provide my son with a respectable position, but instead his
work dishonors us. We use the expression, 'Noble hunger outweighs
ignoble satiation.' Ibn Tulun pressed her to explain. She replied: 'My
son, and this man is to blame, engages in malicious rumor-mongering
that targets innocent folk — our neighbors shun him. Were it not that
it was other than my son [who is at fault], I would have abandoned
him. Why would I bother? Such behavior deserves nothing less than
the contempt of the Almighty and believers alike.' Ahmad ibn Tulun,
laughing, ordered me to continue paying her son the monthly stipend of
ten *dinars* but excuse him from his duties at the *barid*, which I did. She
praised him generously, saying: 'Governor, this is why we turn to you!'
and departed."

The story has Umm Uqba approach Ibn Tulun twice. His first decision worked out badly through no fault of his own; one reading is
that Uqba, in fact, was to blame. He bungled the job and his mother
stepped in to limit the damage and, on hearing her follow-up complaint, Ibn Tulun resolved matters. The story has him seek an equitable outcome; it has him act out of a sense of right. It is precisely
here where the challenge lies in reading the medieval sources in their
rendering of Ibn Tulun's career.

The story cannot be checked. It provides what scholars refer to
as "an impression of factuality": it seems to recount a real event, but
nothing can be done to corroborate it. The problem of historicity even
goes to Umm Uqba and her son, about whom no other information
exists. More can be said of the other actors, Ibn Tulun, clearly, but
also Ibn Aslam and Ibn Muhajir, both of whom are known members of
the Tulunid administration. But, of the part played in this one episode
by all five persons, there is no way to judge. These reports, in the
way of all clever stories, are highly fashioned. They rely on various
types of literary devices; they often stand on their own with little connection to other stories; their origin ("authorship") is difficult to pin
down; and they undergo reshaping as they drift from source to source.
Al-Balawi sought to distinguish his project from that of Ibn al-Daya,
and did so, it seems, by reframing many of the *akhbar* that he drew
from his predecessor. Our story is a case in point.

To set the stories aside, however, would mean the loss of valuable references. The medieval writers were close observers of contemporary society. The story of Umm Uqba, for example, refers to the *barid*, a branch of Tulunid governance. The indication is not only that the Tulunids relied on intelligence gathering, but that the *barid* was held in low regard. Seeking law and order, Tulunid agents probably crossed the line from policing to repression, a pattern all too familiar in non-elite urban neighborhoods. The story likely sheds light, in other words, on one facet of relations between the Tulunid state and the Egyptian populace.

These references can be joined to other information on Tulunid governance. So, for example, the story assumes, more generally, the presence of functioning administrative structures under Ibn Tulun's leadership, in this case of the security services. And it is fortunate that we possess non-literary forms of evidence, including coins, documents, and such physical structures as Ibn Tulun's mosque and the remains of an aqueduct. Such material evidence helps in checking the "literary" clues. Numismatists use coinage, for example, to determine the chronology of Tulunid rule and shifts in its administrative history. The biographies speak to Ibn Tulun's fiscal policies and, at least in some cases, the written accounts sit well with the material evidence.

The biographies, in sum, are no simple collections of stories. But there is a further wrinkle. It concerns each author's intent. In representing Ibn Tulun, the accounts join two streams of Arabic-Islamic writing: biography and advice literature. The aim of the latter type of writing was to provide guidance to persons in office or, in more general terms, commentary on political authority. These works speak to ideals of governance. Modern readers might see this as political "spin": Ibn al-Daya and al-Balawi use their respective accounts of Ibn Tulun's career to contribute to contemporary political debate. Consider, again, the story of Umm Uqba. It has Ibn Tulun, responding to her petitions, reach an equitable solution. He does so in a display of authority and level-headedness, leavened with a sympathetic view of his subjects (the Egyptian people), and, not least of all, a sense of humor.

The story assigns these qualities to the governor. But was Ibn Tulun a useful foil? Or was he simply one power broker among many, acting mostly to promote his own interests? Much turns on how one reads the biographies. The authors present him as a principled actor, whose conduct went beyond mere posturing: he looked beyond self-interest, that is, his own prestige, authority, and wealth. Over and again, the biographers comment on the principles of justice, piety, and charity that informed the *amir*'s conduct. But it is striking too that neither biographer shies from raising critical questions of Ibn Tulun's leadership. This is, in any case, one reading of passages that portray, for example, Ibn Tulun debating interlocutors on the proper use of public moneys or governance itself. Ibn Tulun, as an example of the "good prince," crafted a new political program of which an appeal to Islamic sensibilities was a vital ingredient. But did he do so perfectly? The answer is that he did not. A useful foil, to be sure, he nonetheless fell short of the biographers' ideal.

Thus, the story has Ibn Tulun appoint Uqba not because he was suited for office – it seems he was not – but as a favor to his mother. Was it a case of nepotism? The story also hints at a wider critique. It goes to Umm Uqba's complaint: was Ibn Tulun monitoring Egypt's population unduly? Was he, in other words, abusing his authority? The sources raise the question more pointedly in dealing with the governor's treatment of (perceived) critics. Ibn al-Daya states that 18,000 individuals perished in Ibn Tulun's custody. Among them were persons held in Ibn Tulun's palace; others were consigned to al-Mutbaq, Ibn Tulun's notorious prison. Later sources repeat the same remark. To focus on the number, implausibly large, would be to miss the point. At issue, or so it seems, was Ibn Tulun's turn to repression, that is, overreach on the governor's part. A firm hand was one thing, harsh retribution quite another. On this count, Ibn Tulun stood to be corrected.

The point is that the biographers worked with what either they or their informants witnessed of Ibn Tulun's tenure in office. His opinions, decisions, actions, and policies: this was the "raw material" with which the writers fashioned a description of Ibn Tulun in his capacity as governor and dynast.

EGYPT AND THE SAMARRAN COMMAND

Before turning to Ibn Tulun's approach to governance, a further comment is in order on his initial appointment. The context has been discussed already: the emergence of the Turkic-Central Asian command in Samarra. Bayakbak, to whom Ibn Tulun owed his initial assignment, and Yarjukh, his father-in-law and the person responsible for Ibn Tulun's reappointment, were members of this select circle. Though neither man remained long on the scene, their assignment over Egypt is evidence of their standing.

The commanders, particularly in their role as vice-regents, owed much to Abbasid patronage. The imperial court and military hierarchy provided the officers with considerable material support: top salaries, gifts of slave women (wives and concubines), urban properties and rural estates, high-level appointments and, generally, a seat at the imperial decision-making table. Patronage operated in the Abbasid Empire as the grease of social mobility. It follows that the Samarran command had every reason to see to the survival of the imperial state. But these dynamics were hardly static. The commanders, as their careers progressed, gained sets of interests – wealth and authority – that they worked hard to protect. These efforts were an important driver of the violence in Samarra. Such were the rules of the game: to remain a passive recipient of imperial largesse was to court political ruin.

Wealth, connections, and prestige in hand, the commanders were now also in a position to offer patronage of their own, as illustrated by Yarjukh's reappointment of Ibn Tulun. This is to see authority as having shifted in good measure from the Abbasid court to the military command, with the imperial court now having to share governance over a troubled empire. The same "Samarran" dynamics, however, fueled internecine conflict: the commanders vied for influence and office. The resulting upheaval engulfed the capital, Samarra, and soon spilled into the provinces.

The sources speak to the impact of these developments on Ibn Tulun's career, referring, for example, to his aversion to his fellow "Turks." But, more to the point, they underscore Ibn Tulun's ability to exploit the opportunities at hand. It meant, in part, an effort at shaping a network of support, in Egypt and Samarra alike. At issue as well was the rivalry with al-Muwaffaq, which can only have fueled the same effort. Ibn Tulun relied on contacts with high-level merchants, officials and bureaucrats in Iraq and, especially, long-term relationships with select members of the Turkic-Central Asian military. Tayfur al-Turki was one such figure: Ibn Tulun's biographers, as seen below, make much of his activity in Samarra on behalf of the governor.

A key point in this context is that the Samarran commanders likely saw Egypt as a critical interest. It stands to reason: Egypt was second only to Iraq as a source of revenue, and much prestige attached to its governance. Ibn al-Daya and al-Balawi appear to have understood things precisely in these terms. Al-Balawi, for his part, provides a list of the governors appointed to Egypt by the first four of Samarra's caliphs, beginning with al-Mu'tasim. In nearly all cases, the appointees were prominent members of the Turkic-Central Asian command. The list concludes with Ibn Tulun. The sources never state it expressly, but there is reason to think that he arrived in al-Fustat with marching orders in hand. He was to sustain the military command's grip on Egypt and its considerable revenue stream.

Circumstances, however, allowed Ibn Tulun to move many steps further. It is useful to recall that he took office at a point of grim transition: the once formidable Arab-Islamic Empire was unraveling. The ingredients of disintegration included the loss of caliphal authority. In Samarra, al-Mu'tamid, young and untested, confronted the ambitions of al-Muwaffaq and, in Egypt, those of Ibn Tulun. In practical terms, caliph, regent, and governor had become contestants of equal standing. The Abbasid house would hold the throne for centuries to come and, in that capacity, wield considerable symbolic authority at the head of the Islamic "community" (Ar., *umma*). But, beginning late in the Samarra period, the caliphs slowly lost hold of their part in decision-making, specifically the command of armies, the allocation of fiscal wealth, and the appointment of high-level officials. These matters fell to civilian and military actors, men like Ibn Tulun in the case of Egypt.

But Ibn Tulun – as exemplar – had to justify his conduct in office. He had little legitimate claim to the sort of authority wielded, for example, by the caliphs. In shaping claims to a new style of author-ity, he turned to a variety of public gestures, pronouncements, and policies, what might be thought of as a "repertoire" of power. Such gestures included the ouster of Shuqayr and Ibn Mudabbir, and the public ceremonies following the suppression of the uprisings in the Delta and Upper Egypt. But these measures only paved the way. Ibn Tulun had also to govern. This chapter focuses on three pillars of his nascent state: his large household; the military and security services; and his control over Egypt's fiscal administration.

FAMILY AND HOUSEHOLD

The term "household" typically designates immediate kin: the rela-tionships of blood and marriage joining a power broker to his closest relatives. As a large and unwieldy venue, Ibn Tulun's house appears to have been typical. But historians also use "household" for wider cir-cles held together by relationships of mutual benefit. Political, social, and economic interests either replaced or worked alongside blood and marriage. These were personal ties, each a spoke in a socio-political wheel with, in the case of Ibn Tulun, the *amir* as its axis.

Ibn Tulun, as seen already, was himself the product of such relation-ships. He had drawn as a young officer on the support of his father's household. Al-Balawi, in his opening section on Ibn Tulun's early years, refers briefly to a certain Yalbakh, describing him as a jovial fellow, a fine singer and a close companion of Ibn Tulun's father. On the latter's death in 854, Yalbakh took Ibn Tulun in hand, a favor that Ibn Tulun would repay a decade later, following Yalbakh's death, in providing for his wife and daughter. This goes to Ibn Tulun's relations with his fellow Samarran "Turks." While he may have thought little of his peers, his ties to Yalbakh and others of the Samarran military, notably Bayakbak and Yarjukh, suggest it was more a matter of choice: Ibn Tulun's attachments in Samarra were select but crucial, and the *amir* paid them close attention.

There were, in addition, Ibn Tulun's first connections to the Abbasid court. It is difficult to know what to make of Ibn Tulun's ties to al-Musta'in. The latter's arrest, exile, and execution in 865–866 were dealt with earlier. The biographers indicate that relations with the unfortunate caliph provided Ibn Tulun with an early career boost. Ibn Tulun's later connections with the court of al-Mu'tamid were of a different sort, in that the *amir* had become a powerful figure in his own right. The point is that Ibn Tulun's contacts in Samarra extended deep into the imperial palace.

The benefits and headaches of large households and networks worked in equal measure. Ibn Tulun's dealings with Yarjukh's family are a case in point. Al-Balawi indicates that the *amir*'s one-time patron, dead in 872, left seven children. Yarjukh had married his sole daughter (unnamed) to Musa ibn Bugha, Ibn Tulun's one-time challenger. (The impact on the marriage of Ibn Bugha's aborted campaign against Egypt is left unexplained.) Following his father's death, Isa, the eldest of the six sons, made little effort to provide for the family; al-Balawi refers to him as self-centered. Following a petition on Isa's part, Ibn Tulun brought the family to Egypt. He then arranged, among other steps, the marriage of his daughter, Fatima bint Khatun, to Yarjukh's second son, Ja'far. Neither of the two brothers, however, proved particularly grateful. Al-Balawi has Isa malign the governor in some manner of public statement. Ibn Tulun, with uncharacteristic patience, allowed Isa to transfer (alone) to Tarsus. Ja'far ibn Yarjukh, for his part, frequented the company of al-Abbas and was exiled following the latter's failed rebellion.

How did Ibn Tulun manage his own household? His immediate family consisted of his wives, concubines, siblings, and offspring. It seems that neither of Ibn Tulun's parents joined him in Egypt. And only one collective reference exists to the women of Ibn Tulun's house. It says that al-Mu'tamid, acting perhaps on al-Muwaffaq's urging, made an early attempt to remove Ibn Tulun from office. The *amir* responded with gifts sent with the ever-loyal Ahmad al-Wasiti. The effort succeeded, and the decision was reversed. Al-Wasiti used the occasion to secure the transfer of Ibn Tulun's women and offspring to Egypt. Had the governor's family been held in Iraq as a source of leverage? This is unclear; imperial appointees perhaps left their dependants at home for the duration of their tours in office. Ibn Tulun's ability to secure the transfer of his family speaks, in any case, to his contacts in Samarra.

The passage does not name the Tulunid women, but there are other references. In addition to Khatun, Yarjukh's daughter, one reads of Mayyas, an enslaved woman (Ar., *jariya*), given to Ibn Tulun by al-Musta'in, and Na't, described as Ibn Tulun's *umm walad*, a legal term designating the concubine mother of a master's child. Na't occurs among Ibn al-Daya's many informants. Al-Balawi also refers in passing to Asma, describing her as "a freedman's daughter married to Ibn Tulun in Egypt." The account has Ibn Tulun, worried lest she pass on her slight features to (male) offspring, use coitus interruptus when sleeping with her. (The reference suggests a considerable age difference between governor and his new wife.) The three references point, among other things, to the role that enslaved and freed women played in elite households, that of the Tulunids included.

Khatun (al-Abbas and Fatima), Mayyas (Khumarawayh), and Na't (Abu al-Asha'ir), all bore Ibn Tulun's children. The governor had thirty-three offspring in all, sixteen of them girls. Fatima is named only in passing, as are Rabi'a and Nasr among his sons. Another son, Adnan ibn Ahmad ibn Tulun, achieved a degree of prominence as a religious scholar (as seen below). What impact did al-Abbas's revolt have on Khatun's fortunes? And how did Mayyas's life change when Ibn Tulun tapped Khumarawayh as heir? The sources are silent. They also say nothing of relations among the Tulunid women themselves; one can assume that differences of age, ethnic background, and temperament, not to speak of such developments as al-Abbas's revolt, shaped these relations. Elite women took part in court politics across Near Eastern history. Examples include the Prophet's wives in seventh-century Medina; ranking women of the tenth-century Abbasid caliphate; and queen mothers of the later Seljuq and Ottoman dynasties. It was often a matter of securing high office for favorite sons; the women of the Tulunid court may well have pursued the same aim but, unfortunately, the biographers say almost nothing on this score.

Information on the males of the Tulunid household is, unsurprisingly, much richer. The best such information concerns Ibn Tulun's brother, Musa, and al-Abbas, his eldest son. Khumarawayh appears in the sources mostly after his appointment as heir. The impact of

Ibn Tulun's confrontation with al-Abbas was profound. Indications include an angry letter to his son, preserved by al-Balawi, in which the governor speaks in good part as a father: unless his son sought forgiveness, he, the *amir*, had little option but to repudiate his family ties. Ibn Tulun defused his son's challenge, as seen already, but the crisis was a serious distraction at a point when money, troops, and political capital were needed elsewhere. Al-Abbas's subsequent murder was probably ordered by Khumarawayh; the two men were rivals, first, kinsmen, second.

As for Musa, al-Kindi, a key Egyptian source, indicates that Ibn Tulun relied on his brother early on, appointing him over the *shurta* – the police force – and, later, as deputy governor during the aborted campaign into Syria in 870. Musa insisted on a greater share in governance, however, at which point Ibn Tulun balked. A crisis erupted following Ibn Tulun's assignment to Alexandria. Musa asked to be appointed over the city and, on his brother's refusal, raged at Ibn Tulun in open court. The latter responded by exiling Musa to Tarsus. Musa rejected subsequent conciliatory gestures on his brother's part, including formal appointment over the frontier city. Ibn al-Daya's informant in this case – Musa's son, Muhammad – was a third generation Tulunid; the passage extends Musa little sympathy, yet further indication of Tulunid family tensions.

Al-Balawi describes al-Abbas's revolt as marking a sharp slide in Ibn Tulun's authority. This seems off: there is reason to think that the *amir* used the occasion to strengthen relations with his military command. But, needless to say, neither of the two confrontations – with Musa and al-Abbas – can have done much for the cohesion of the Tulunid house. A third episode, Lu'lu''s defection, had yet a deeper impact. To briefly sum up, Ibn Tulun had posted Lu'lu', his long-standing client, to the Jazira at the conclusion of the second Syrian campaign in 877. Lu'lu', pressed by his secretary, Ibn Sulayman, and after seizing revenue normally bound for Egypt, led his troops into Iraq, where they were immediately used by al-Muwaffaq against the Zanj. Ibn Tulun then responded with his final Syrian campaign in 883–884. Lu'lu''s decision was a blow on several fronts. His units, among the finest in Ibn Tulun's army, were now lost to the *amir* as was the revenue from the provinces of the Jazira assigned to Lu'lu'. There was, of course, also the political fallout: al-Muwaffaq, in drawing Lu'lu' to his side, won a significant round against Ibn Tulun.

Lu'lu's biography – which exists only in fragments – offers a three-fold lesson on the organization and dynamics of medieval Near Eastern households. First, there is the ubiquitous presence of enslaved and freed persons, males and females alike. As just noted, concubines figured importantly among the women of the Tulunid house. Of the many unfree or freed males in Ibn Tulun's inner circle, alongside Lu'lu', there were Nasim and Badr al-Kabir al-Hamami (d. 923–924). A second lesson concerns the opportunity for social advancement that integration into elite households offered such persons. Lu'lu' is one example: al-Balawi describes him as having become a mainstay of Ibn Tulun's polity. Nasim, for his part, was, like Lu'lu', a *khadim* or eunuch. One measure of Nasim's standing lies in the many references to him as an informant; he spoke often, it seems, to Ibn al-Daya and perhaps al-Balawi as well. These references indicate a long-standing relationship with Ibn Tulun. He was on hand at the onset of the governor's tenure; he carried out numerous duties on his master's behalf; and attended Ibn Tulun on his deathbed. As for Badr, he is spoken of by various sources as having been a Greek (Byzantine) slave and one of Ibn Tulun's freedmen (Ar., *mawali*). He was to gain particular stature in the period following Ibn Tulun's death.

The third lesson concerns loyalty, the binding element of these elite households. Loyalty acted as assurance that services would be carried out and the interests of the house properly represented. Client relations mattered nearly as much as blood ties. Of the three cases of internal rupture – Ibn Tulun's confrontations with, respectively, Musa, al-Abbas, and Lu'lu' – the one to which Ibn Tulun reacted with greatest urgency was the last. The circumstances, it is true, demanded a particularly strong response. But al-Balawi suggests that Ibn Tulun took the defection as much to heart as his son's uprising. The reaction, in one sense, was personal. The governor, in a letter to Lu'lu', addressed his wayward client in deeply familiar terms. But his pained response had to do with a good deal more: Lu'lu', in throwing off relations with the Tulunid house, undercut the rules of loyalty, trust, and patronage that informed elite politics. This reflected on Lu'lu', certainly, but on Ibn Tulun as well. The governor's end goal was the legitimation of authority, a project that turned on a demonstrated understanding of proper governance. Lu'lu's conduct, in this sense, left him little option but to respond vigorously. To ignore it would have meant a serious slip in reputation.

Ibn Tulun's household included other sectors of Egyptian society more generally. These wider networks are difficult to describe in detail; the biographies' narrow focus on the *amir* means that even leading members of the Tulunid court appear only when interacting directly with the governor. These contacts were numerous and of a great variety. His relations with the military command will be treated below. His civilian contacts included landowners and merchants, local and Abbasid-level courtiers, scribes, bureaucrats, and poets.

The members of this last category were mostly local figures, with little of the standing of the great Abbasid court poets. Poets had long served in Near Eastern courts, in part, as propagandists; Ibn Tulun knew to use them in this capacity. If surviving examples of their verse are a reliable guide, they provided Ibn Tulun with appropriate expressions of veneration. The sources name two poets – Qa'dan ibn Amr and Munsif ibn Khalifa al-Hudhali – among others. Al-Kindi quotes al-Hudhali: Ibn Tulun was that "most excellent man of this world." More telling still is Qa'dan ibn Amr's reference to the *amir* as rightly inspired:

Divine guidance extends from the *amir* Ibn Tulun,
Much as religion itself flourishes through him,
Why, even beyond religion and Islam.

Persons in other categories of Ibn Tulun's civilian network stand out. Ahmad al-Wasiti appears first in the sources in connection with al-Musta'in's execution. The passage, in which he assists Ibn Tulun in shrouding the caliph's body, refers to him as a *ghulam*, a term meaning both "young man" and "male slave"; he may have been among Ibn Tulun's household freedmen. He remained at his side from that point forward, carrying out a series of high-level duties. Things, however, ultimately went sour: al-Balawi's last reference to al-Wasiti describes his decision to abandon Khumarawayh following Ibn Tulun's death.

The sources also speak of Tukhshi ibn Balbard's years of service to Ibn Tulun. His example reminds us that the division between "military" and "civilian" was blurred: Tukhshi held both sorts of offices. Ibn Tulun assigned him, for example, to govern Tarsus after Musa ibn Tulun refused that same office. A letter on papyrus survives in which a scribe in Tukhshi's employ refers to his administration of the estates of Tukhshi's children, a suggestion of the rewards enjoyed by the father for his years of service in the Tulunid administration. Ibn Tulun also employed Tukhshi's brother, Ibrahim, as head of the *shurta*.

Many of Ibn Tulun's associates also served the governor as conduits of information. Tayfur al-Turki, Ibn Tulun's deputy, resided in Iraq, from where he kept Ibn Tulun informed on developments at the Abbasid court. At one juncture, Tayfur frustrated al-Muwaffaq's efforts at finding a replacement for Ibn Tulun, an effort that culminated in Musa ibn Bugha's aborted march on Egypt. On each occasion that al-Muwaffaq offered Egypt to a new candidate, usually a ranking member of the military, Tayfur arrived with a bribe large enough to convince the individual in question to think again.

Ma`mar al-Jawhari ("the Jeweler"), a prominent merchant, is said to have been on particularly intimate terms with Ibn Tulun; upon Ma`mar's death, the *amir* is said to have collapsed in grief. Anecdotes speak of his many contacts in Iraq – a brother, also a jewel merchant, lived in Baghdad – and the services that he provided the *amir* there and in Egypt. He was, for example, among four notables dispatched by Ibn Tulun to al-Abbas in the failed attempt to curtail the latter's rebellion.

Ibn Tulun also sought to create a cadre of Egyptian officials. References point to a policy of recruiting local figures although Ibn Tulun continued to employ Iraqi officials as well. The governor was less successful, however, in winning over Egypt's religious scholars. The sources speak of Ibn Tulun's generosity toward the religious establishment, including gifts to visiting scholars and support to Qur'an-reciters and jurists. The new mosque can be seen as a further gesture. But these relations grew uneasy, as seen in Ibn Tulun's dealings with Bakkar ibn Qutayba. These will be treated later; suffice it here to say that the confrontation of governor and judge had two emergent power circles of Near Eastern society take the measure of each other.

Households were, in sum, a central institution of ninth-century public life, and Ibn Tulun's attention to his own sprawling networks was typical. Also typical were efforts by Ibn Tulun and his peers to target rival networks. He and al-Muwaffaq confronted one another often through proxies, among them spies, envoys, and field commanders. Households/networks were fair game as instruments and targets alike. But how were they maintained? The key was generosity, one of the ingredients that defined sound leadership. It was a matter of the appropriate use of public wealth; appointments to office; forms of social bonding including marriage; and a variety of ceremonial gestures, including formal vows. Ibn Tulun's biographers would have us believe that the *amir* knew the value of each such ingredient.

THE TULUNID ARMY AND POLICE

A full history of the Tulunid military is beyond our grasp. No formal archives remain, apart from scattered papyrus documents, and the written sources are disinterested in Tulunid military affairs per se. Relevant information also needs to be used with care; troop numbers, for example, often seem exaggerated. What is clear is that Ibn Tulun established a large and complex security-military establishment. And, as seen below, Ibn Tulun devoted much care to nurturing his ties to the military command, often in the form of public ceremony.

To consider Ibn Tulun's military build-up, a brief comment on the history of Arab-Islamic forces in Egypt is in order. Into the mid-eighth century, these forces consisted predominantly of Arab tribal units, known as the *jund*. These forces settled in Egypt on the heels of the Arab-Islamic conquest and were commanded by Arab tribal chiefs. These men typically headed up the *shurta* as well and thus assumed responsibility for the pay rosters. The civil war that brought al-Ma'mun to power, at the turn of the ninth century, saw imperial control over

Egypt nearly collapse. The Abbasid state, anxious to control Egypt's wealth, dispatched largely Iranian and Central Asian units to the Nile Valley. This step, and a complex local power struggle, led to a sharp decline in the cohesion and authority of the Arab-dominated *jund*.

A third overlapping chapter ensued with the ascension of al-Mu'ta-sim, and the appearance of the Turkic-Central Asian military. This was the context, of course, of Ibn Tulun's eventual appointment. A key moment occurred in 838: according to al-Kindi, the new caliph – Abu Ishaq al-Mu'tasim – ordered the last Arab units of the *jund* to be removed from the imperial pay register (Ar., *diwan*). This was all part of the consolidation by the Turkic-Central Asian military presence in the Nile Valley. It involved a steady influx of Samarran units and personnel, a process that is difficult to track though the indications are clear of a predominant Turkic military presence in Egypt at the moment of Ibn Tulun's arrival.

A description of the Tulunid security and military establishment begins with two offices: the *barid* and, again, the *shurta*. The first of these, referenced in the Umm Uqba story, was a long-standing insti-tution in the Arab-Islamic Empire, with origins in the pre-Islamic Near East. It functioned in part as a postal system: much official com-munication flowed, particularly to and from the Abbasid center. But the *barid* also handled intelligence, information on which leaders, Ibn Tulun included, relied in monitoring local and regional developments. We have seen that Ibn Tulun took control of the office after ousting Shuqayr, the once-powerful head of the office. The biographies refer frequently to intelligence-gathering and related activity – exchanges of letters, gifts, and bribes – on the part of both Ibn Tulun and his Abbasid opponents. These included efforts by al-Muwaffaq to plant spies in al-Qata'i'; in a series of stories, Ibn Tulun, ever alert, identi-fies in each case the individual in question and has him punished. More than mere stories, these likely reflect a pattern of Tulunid history.

Information and punishment – arrest, imprisonment, public humil-iation, torture, and execution – were instruments at Ibn Tulun's dis-posal and which he typically assigned to the *shurta*. The sources, as noted earlier, refer to the large numbers of persons that lingered, and often perished, in al-Mutbaq – the main prison in al-Qata'i' – as well as Ibn Tulun's own palace. Al-Balawi refers frequently to imprisoned persons. These anecdotes, typically, have Ibn Tulun summon individuals from their cells for questioning, often in public sessions. These appear as one form of ceremony in which intimidation, of the imprisoned and the populace at large, was as much an aim as the questioning itself.

Bakkar ibn Qutayba, the chief judge, was the best known of these individuals, persons we would know today as political prisoners. The relationship of the two men, as seen earlier, broke down at the Damascus Assembly in 883. There are indications of other sources of tension between the two men as well, as in two brief anecdotes in which Bakkar refused petitions by the Tulunid administration to seize lands that had been designated as religious properties. Such tensions, one thinks, were politically awkward: relations with the Islamic religious establishment were never far from Ibn Tulun's mind and Bakkar, by virtue of his office, was its most prominent representative. It is telling, both of the delicacy of the relationship and, perhaps, of Bakkar's own personality, that when Ibn Tulun offered to release the elderly jurist, the latter refused, citing his determination to heed only divine judgment. The likelihood is that Bakkar, for all his studied piety, knew to use his own example to embarrass Ibn Tulun politically.

The second office, the *shurta*, was an equally well-established branch of imperial rule. An elite military office, its responsibilities included the assurance of law and order – hence the term is often translated as "police" – as well as protection of the governor and his household. The holder of the office, the *sahib al-shurta*, had come in earlier periods of Egypt's Islamic history from prominent local Arab families. In most cases, the individual had been an appointee of the governor, although at different points one family held the office over several generations. Ibn Tulun, in appointing the *sahib al-shurta*, continued where his immediate predecessors left off in selecting Turkic-Central Asian officers instead, a further indication of the Samarran military presence in Egypt. Al-Kindi names a series of these individuals: Buzan al-Turki, Musa ibn Tawniq, Tughlugh, Tukhshi ibn Balbard, Muhammad ibn Harthama, al-Hasan ibn Ghalib al-Tarsusi, Ibrahim ibn Balbard (Tukhshi's brother), and Sari ibn Sahl. (Again, the reading of such names is uncertain.) Several of these men led units in the field as well at different points. Ibn Tulun, with these appointments, was likely pursuing two aims: on the one hand, serving the interest in Egypt on the part of the Samarran command and, on the other, consolidating his own relations with the local military hierarchy.

The one point is worth stressing: few if any of these men were of local origin. As modern scholars have suggested, the Abbasid caliphate, in recruiting troops from eastern Iran and the frontiers of Central Asia, grew ever more reliant on forces that were culturally and linguistically distinct from local populations that included, in many areas, majority non-Muslim communities. That outsiders dominated the security and fiscal affairs of, in this case, Egypt, can only have exacerbated socio-political divisions, both within the province and empire wide.

There is much to suggest the appearance of such divisions under Ibn Tulun. The *amir*, for example, made every effort to stamp out local opposition. It was an effort at securing a monopoly of force. So, for example, we have considered the campaign of "pacification" carried out by Tulunid forces in the first half of the *amir*'s reign, against Ibn Tabataba, Ibn al-Sufi, al-Umari, Abu Ruh, and the populace of Barqa. In each case, it was a matter of bringing outlying regions of Egypt to heel. Many details are missing, but each episode likely involved resistance to the fiscal and political control of al-Fustat. As such, they were of a piece with long-standing resistance in Egypt to imperial – Umayyad and Abbasid – authority. An ingredient of each episode is likely to have been resentment at the authority of outsiders, including, significantly, Ibn Tulun himself. Information considered later suggests that the *amir* sought to address these same resentments.

Turning to the Tulunid military more generally, a starting point is a description provided by Ibn al-Daya. A list of the resources that Ibn Tulun bequeathed to Khumarawayh includes troops, livestock, and ships as well as major defensive projects, including the fortress on the island of Rawda. It refers specifically to a register containing the names of 7,000 freedmen (Ar., *mawali*) and 24,000 slave troops (Ar., *ghilman*). Al-Maqrizi – who likely drew on al-Balawi's *Sira* though he does not say so directly – refers to Ibn Tulun's army as made up of the "foreign-born" (Ar., *ajam*) and freedmen/slaves (Ar., *mawali*). He says: "the numbers of slaves grew excessive, exceeding 24,000 Turkish slaves (Ar., *ghulam*), 40,000 blacks, and 7,000 salaried free soldiers." This last group consisted probably of mercenaries.

What to make of this information? The numbers themselves are problematic. This goes as well to al-Kindi's reference to a force of 100,000 troops that Ibn Tulun sent to contain al-Abbas's revolt; other sources use a similar number if in different contexts. The best reading is that numbers, rounded off as they so often are in our sources, were meant to signal the scale of Ibn Tulun's military build-up. Few references, unfortunately, speak of the command structure of the Tulunid armies. To get at a better overall description, we might consider two rough categories of Tulunid forces, then return to the military command.

In the first category were the imperial forces at Ibn Tulun's disposal upon his arrival, that is, forces built up prior to his tenure. The information on these forces is fragmentary but telling. Al-Balawi states that Bayakbak assigned Ibn Tulun an army (Ar., *jaysh*) but provides no further detail. Given that it accompanied Ibn Tulun from Iraq, and given the Samarran military's long connection to Egypt, it seems likely that it consisted of mounted Turkic-Central Asian units, including individuals that had served with Ibn Tulun along the Byzantine frontier. In the same category were the forces on the ground upon his arrival in 868. These were probably the units led by Buhm ibn al-Husayn, Lu'lu', and other officers in the campaigns against Ibn Tabataba and other local opponents. These units, it is safe to say, consisted chiefly of troops of Turkic or Central Asian descent. There is unfortunately no information on hand regarding native Egyptian troops, interactions among the different forces, and how Ibn Tulun organized his military once in office (i.e. through training, outfitting, billeting and so on).

It was, it seems, only several years after his arrival in al-Fustat that Ibn Tulun initiated a military build-up. This goes to the second broad element of the Tulunid army. There is a small question as where to include the Afghani (Ghur) guardsmen that Ibn Tulun acquired from Ibn al-Mudabbir. This was a small unit of 100 men, and the indications are that the *amir* used them in ceremonial fashion. The sources say little about them in any case. More significant were the units created by Ibn Tulun in the context of his campaign against Isa ibn al-Shaykh.

To briefly recap, Ibn al-Shaykh, seeking to capitalize on the upheaval in Samarra, made a bid for control of Syria in 870. To recruit his own fighters, Ibn al-Shaykh confiscated Egyptian revenue bound for Samarra. An offer of a negotiated settlement rejected, al-Mu'tamid ordered Ibn Tulun to march on Ibn al-Shaykh. The campaign ended with news of the arrival of Amajur in Damascus. Ibn Tulun, using revenue provided him by Ibn al-Mudabbir (as per imperial instructions), had acted quickly, however, in forming new infantry units. It is upon his return to al-Fustat that Ibn Tulun ordered the construction of al-Qata'i', in good part to accommodate the new units.

Ibn al-Daya refers to them as "the Red and Black." Al-Balawi is more specific: "slaves – Byzantines (Ar., *Rum*) and blacks (Ar., *Sudan*)." Unfortunately, neither author provides further detail; they say nothing of the specific origins of either the "Red" (i.e. Byzantine) or "Black" troops, nor by what channels Ibn Tulun acquired them. A passing mention by Qa'dan ibn Amr, the Tulunid poet introduced earlier, confirms the presence of both "white" and "black" troops. Using ethnically coded biblical terms, as Michael Bonner has pointed out, Ibn Amr refers to the former as "lofty nobles from the sons of Shem," the latter as "lions from the sons of Ham."

The African troops, acquired in all likelihood from trade routes linking Egypt, the Red Sea, and the East African coast, appear several times in the sources. Unlike the Samarran Turkic and Central Asian soldiers, they do so as an anonymous mass, with no provision of individual names, sense of specific origins, or achievements in the field. According to various references, the black troops were targeted specifically by Abbasid troops in 905 during the assault on the Tulunid state. Again, however, no explanation is provided. The sources say even less about the "white" or Byzantine units. *The History of the Patriarchs of Alexandria*, an Arabic-language Coptic text, refers to repeated clashes in the later ninth century, mostly at sea, between "the Muslims and the Greeks," in which "great numbers" of captives were seized by each side. This suggests a market in Byzantine slaves but, again, the sources say nothing that connects it directly to Tulunid recruitment efforts.

How were the slave troops acquired? What training did they undergo? How were the new units structured and paid? The sources offer no answers. In creating the new forces, Ibn Tulun did duplicate an Abbasid pattern of recruiting slave forces. The outcome was similar: the creation of a polyglot military wholly dependent on state salaries and support. There is evidence of a divergence in standing of different Tulunid units: the slave troops (Ar., *ghilman*, *abid*) are referred to alongside the infantry (Ar., *rijal*). Neither appears to have been mounted, setting them apart from the Turkic-Central Asian forces, who appear to have been cavalry. Related references, notably in regard to al-Qata'i`, suggest that Ibn Tulun, like his Abbasid counterparts, struggled with problems of discipline, perhaps another indication of the complexity in makeup of the Tulunid military.

The indications of a Tulunid military build-up are clear. But, initially, it may have come as a *reaction* to events. There is reason to argue, in other words, that the aborted effort to subdue Ibn al-Shaykh prompted Ibn Tulun to consider expansion into Syria and thus the build-up itself. (If he gave short shrift to the *risks* of such expansion, he was not the first Egyptian strongman to do so, nor the last.) And the new forces did impose fiscal and political demands on his administration. Tensions arose upon the arrival in al-Fustat of the new, foreign units; these led to their relocation to al-Qata'i`. And the new forces appear to have created other headaches as well. The fourteenth-century Christian Palestinian source, the *Continuatio*, describes Tulunid forces on campaign later in Syria. It refers specifically to pillaging and other acts carried out by "the black soldiers" against the Syrian populace and local properties.

Better information on Tulunid military history concerns Ibn Tulun's officer corps. Among them were field commanders – Lu'lu', up to the point of his defection, is a case in point – and individuals, including Tukhshi ibn Balbard, with both military and civilian assignments. Judging, again, by their names, it seems few of these men were Egyptian by origin or, indeed, speaking of the first generation, Near

Eastern. Only a few of the names indicates that they were first- (or second-) generation Muslims, as in the case of Buhm ibn al-Husayn or Ahmad ibn Jayghawayh. The names of other commanders are wholly ambiguous on this score; Shu'ba ibn Kharkan al-Babaki; Yalbaq al-Tarsusi; Yazbak al-Farghani; and Abu al-Aswad al-Ghitrif.

Relations with his commanders were never far from Ibn Tulun's mind. There is reason to think that while Ibn Tulun arrived in Egypt with an army in hand and strong support from elements of the Samarran military, he still had need to cultivate relations with the officer corps in Egypt. He did so, as seen earlier, with a mix of ceremony and patronage, including the gifting of horses, robes, and fine belts. A second point is that many of the references to his commanders occur in accounts of the campaign against Ibn Tabataba and the other local movements. The sources do not say as much, but the implication is that the Tulunid forces were mounted; they appear, in any case, to have ranged at will between the Delta and Upper Egypt. These offer hints as to the substantial forces at Ibn Tulun's disposal early on: he is said to have quickly dispatched a second army, for example, following an initial rout by his troops at the hands of Ibn al-Sufi.

Ibn Tulun also enhanced the Egyptian navy and Egypt's coastal defenses. Muhammad ibn Da'ud, ever the bitter critic of the Tulunids, provides one reference. In one of several poems, he mocks Ibn Tulun's military build-up, suggesting that his new fleet was intended less to fight the Byzantines than provide the *amir* with the means to take flight (i.e. out of cowardice). The reference is to Ibn Tulun's response to Musa ibn Bugha's campaign. As noted above, he is said to have ordered fortifications built on the island of Rawda and an expansion of the Egyptian fleet. When Ibn Bugha's campaign collapsed, Ibn Tulun cancelled further such efforts, although Ibn al-Daya, in the inventory cited above, refers to 100 warships as among the items bequeathed by Ibn Tulun to Khumarawayh. Nothing is said about the size and capacity of these ships. One view is that the Tulunids established a naval presence across the eastern Mediterranean; the references to Tulunid-Byzantine confrontations at sea supports the point, as does the reference to the fleet that Ibn Tulun sent against the rebellion in Barqa in 875.

THE TULUNID ECONOMY AND ITS ADMINISTRATION

To unlock the puzzle of Ibn Tulun's career, sense has to be made of his fiscal and economic policies. It was a matter, on his part, of securing the resources required to carry out autonomous state-building, including the expansion of his military. The key step, of course, was to deny the Abbasid caliphate unfettered access to Egyptian revenue. To set things in proper context, a discussion of the Tulunid economy follows. Unfortunately, a full such history has yet to be written, although modern scholars, notably Gladys Frantz-Murphy and Kosei Morimoto, have laid significant groundwork. The task is challenging. The written sources provide only fragmentary and, at times, obscure and confusing information. The numismatic, documentary, and archeological record provides invaluable further information and, using such material alongside the written sources, modern historians continue to fit new pieces to the puzzle (and, thus, refit many older pieces in the process). But a full picture remains elusive.

There is good reason to see that Egypt's economy flourished in the Tulunid period. Historians cite indications of robust agrarian production, notably in flax; new levels of commerce in textiles, slaves, and other commodities; and a busy mining sector in gold and other minerals. Documentary information adds to this impression of commercial and agrarian activity, at both the local and regional level, and surviving cloth remnants evince production in textiles and, in particular, *tiraz*, that is, finely woven garments and fabrics (examples of which one can see online in the Metropolitan Museum of Art's collection). Written and numismatic references point to the quality of Tulunid dinars; gold was readily available (as were local skilled die makers). Such information sits well with anecdotal references to, for example, the moneys that al-Abbas coerced from Egypt's merchants to sustain his rebellion; the revenue distributed in Mecca in 883 by Tulunid officers; the large sums that Ibn Tulun bequeathed to Khumarawayh, said to have amounted to ten million *dinars*; and the reported increase in agrarian revenue under Ibn Tulun from 800,000 to well over four million *dinars*.

Further indications include the likely sums required of Ibn Tulun's military build-up and a number of large infrastructure projects. Examples include projects not only in Egypt but in Syria as well. Al-Muqaddasi (d. late tenth century), writing in Palestine, describes a new port that Ibn Tulun ordered built in Acre, a busy coastal town; the *Continuatio*, the Christian source cited earlier, refers to a fortress constructed by Ibn Tulun above Jaffa, also a coastal town; and Ibn Taghribirdi (d. 1470), writing in Egypt, refers to expansion by Ibn Tulun of the tomb complex of Mu`awiya ibn Abi Sufyan, the Umayyad caliph, in Damascus. The list of Tulunid projects in Egypt included, of course, al-Qata'i`, with its imposing new mosque; the aqueduct and hospital; the new palace and expansive plaza; and the extensive barracks and residences that Ibn Tulun had constructed to house his regiments and civilian officials. More will be said of al-Qata'i`, with specific comments on each of these elements, in the next chapter. Here it suffices to point to the considerable expenditures involved in the massive project.

One can point as well to the costs of sustaining a large household. To manage a busy economy, one obvious requirement was a working fiscal administration. There are many indications of just such a system in the Tulunid period. Ibn Tulun, of course, did not fashion it from scratch. It was, rather, the legacy of imperial governance in Egypt over centuries, stretching at least to the Byzantine period. Following the seventh-century conquest of Egypt, the new Arab rulers, in turn, working with local and imperial officials, tax-collectors, landowners, and commanders, developed that same system over many decades. It involved considerable trial and error. Egypt's wealth, in a word, over at least a two-hundred-year history, was exploited by both Umayyad and Abbasid administrations. One has also to account, over this long period, for the effects of civil wars and uprisings, as well as the turn-over and individual whims of governors, tax officials, and other imperial representatives. Ibn Tulun thus had a potent history of government experience and tradition to draw on.

Surviving documents – most written on papyrus – speak to the work of the Tulunid fiscal administration. Three examples serve as illustration; they are among numerous extant Tulunid-era documents. One document, dating to 867, from the province of Ushmun in Middle Egypt, is a tax receipt for estates belonging to elite landowners resident in Iraq. Among the persons named, it appears, is Amajur, the Samarran commander appointed to govern southern Syria in 870. The reference is further indication that a number of Samarran political and military elites controlled properties in Egypt. Among them was also Ibn al-Mudabbir; al-Balawi has the beleaguered tax director offer Ibn Tulun estates as gifts on the eve of his departure from Egypt. A second document, dating to 869–870, records the payment of a poll tax by a Coptic (Christian) resident – a certain Mina ibn Damarqura – in the Fayyum district. And finally, there is a papyrus document dating to 901 containing a set of agreements in which local agents in the small town of Ahnas, located also in the Fayyum, commit to the payment of specific taxes.

The documents, each in their way, point to an extensive fiscal system on which Ibn Tulun could and did rely. To run it, Ibn Tulun relied on tax officials, landowners, security personnel and others at the many levels of government. He administered, in this sense, on a day-to-day basis; the written sources would have us believe that he did so effectively. But the issue at hand concerns Ibn Tulun's political project. Previous governors, including Yazid ibn Abdallah, appear to have governed effectively as well. What changed with Ibn Tulun? What measures, in other words, did the *amir* introduce to assure that Egypt's revenue would serve his ambitions? The question has to do with how he put Egypt's fiscal system to use.

One step, of course, was to suppress local opposition which, in many cases, consisted of tax revolts. As seen earlier, Ibn Tulun responded effectively to the activity of Ibn al-Arqat, Ibn al-Tabataba, Ibn al-Sufi and others, many conducted under the Alid banner. The final effort came against the rebels in Barqa in 875. Seen earlier, as well, was Ibn Tulun's successful effort to win control over the central fiscal offices of Egypt. Ibn Tulun achieved this step by 872 with the ouster of Ibn al-Mudabbir, so roughly four years into his tenure. The biographies indicate that Ibn Tulun, pressed early on by the caliphate for tribute, had complained of having too little influence over Egypt's fiscal affairs. Al-Mu'tamid responded with a high-level delegation, headed by one

Nafis (or Nasim) *al-khadim*, joined by two leading jurists, including the son of Ahmad ibn Hanbal (d. 855), a prominent Baghdadi scholar. They announced – we can imagine a public declaration – Ibn Tulun's appointment over the fiscal administration.

The governor, having taken these steps, was now in position to dictate the flow of Egyptian revenue. To manage it, he grew the provincial state. He is reported to have created a new-style chancellery, for example, an office headed for many years by Muhammad ibn Abd Kan (d. 884). The process, however, is difficult to piece together. It appears that Ibn Tulun relied, in having the Egyptian economy administered, on a combination of Egyptian and Iraqi officials. So, for example, to replace Ibn al-Mudabbir, Ibn Tulun turned initially to a certain Muhammad ibn Hilal, then, sometime later, to Ahmad ibn Muhammad (known also as Ibn Ukht al-Wazir), an obscure figure who held office until his dismissal by Ibn Tulun in 878. Ibn Ukht al-Wazir, it seems, was appointed by al-Mu'tamid, which would indicate that Ibn Tulun welcomed imperial officials to Egypt, this despite tense relations with the Abbasid center. Of the Iraqi officials, the sources also refer to Ishaq ibn Nusayr al-Baghdadi (d. 892), Hasan ibn Muhammad ibn Muhajir and his offspring, and members of the Madhara'i family. The first member of the family, Ahmad ibn Ibrahim (d. 884), replaced Ibn Ukht al-Wazir. His son, Ali ibn Ahmad, went on to head Khumarawayh's administration. His offspring, having survived the Abbasid assault of 905, remained in positions of influence through the tenth century.

Everything points to Ibn Tulun's exacting authority over these officials and, thus, Egypt's fiscal system. This is, in any case, the impression conveyed by Ibn al-Daya and al-Balawi. They have Ibn Tulun, in a series of anecdotes, seeking advice on fiscal matters from officials and advisors before imposing his final say. Ibn Tulun, as governor, seems, in other words, to have enjoyed an unprecedented level of control over the collection and disbursement of revenue. But we want to be sensitive to the way in which Ibn al-Daya and al-Balawi proceed. Take, for example, a story concerning Ma'mar al-Jawhari, Ibn Tulun's long-time ally and friend. The latter lent Ma'mar, a leading merchant, capital to invest in linen which he did successfully. But Ibn

Tulun, acting on some manner of information, came to view these profits as having derived from illicit dealings. He turned to Ibrahim ibn Qiratghan, the official charged with charitable gifts (Ar., *sadaqat*), to confiscate the money in question and redistribute it from his office. The point is not that the governor acted against Ma'mar per se, but that he saw the particular transactions as morally tainted. In correcting a fiscal wrong, Ibn Tulun took the high road, despite having to act against a key supporter.

Another, more pointed story recounts an alleged interview between Ibn Tulun and Abd Allah ibn Dashuma, a ranking finance official. The *amir*, opposed to two sets of supplementary taxes then on the books, decides to abrogate them on grounds that they placed too great a burden on the Egyptian peasantry. The story does not name Ibn al-Mudabbir directly, but there is reason to think that the reference is to the unpopular measures taken by Ibn al-Mudabbir in the period prior to Ibn Tulun's tenure. Ibn Tulun queries Ibn Dashuma on the wisdom of dropping the particular taxes. Ibn Dashuma argues for leaving them in place, describing them as a source of considerable revenue and a potential surplus if and when agrarian production slowed (due, for example, to lower levels of Nile flooding). Ibn Tulun promises to weigh his opinion. That evening, in a dream, he is visited by a former companion from Tarsus, understood to be an ascetic figure and, thus, a source of pious advice. The figure urges him to reject Ibn Dashuma's opinion and thus alleviate his subjects' suffering. Ibn Tulun – brought to his moral senses – cancels both sets of taxes.

The story attaches Ibn Tulun to the frontier ethos of faith and asceticism, all while highlighting his commitment to justice. It then goes on to describe how, upon making his decision, Ibn Tulun was rewarded (as the figure in the dream promised): he stumbles, while hunting the following day, upon an enormous hidden treasure with which he is able to build the new mosque and hospital. Again, Ibn al-Mudabbir seems to lurk in the background, playing the part of the grasping imperial bureaucrat, much like Ibn Dashuma himself. Ibn Tulun, in pushing back, sets right the moral order.

The aim is to pretty up the *amir*'s reputation: he emerges from these accounts as a pious and just reformer. We should react critically.

Such accounts effectively gloss over the very issue under consideration here, Ibn Tulun's determination to have his way with Egypt's revenue for political purposes. The stories of Ibn Tulun's fiscal measures, in other words, can be read as indication of his preoccupation with sound administration. But where questions arise is in relation to his motivations. Modern historians point, for example, to the particular reliance in ninth-century Abbasid Egypt on land contracts. This was a system of revenue collection by which officials and landed elites set terms with the state – the Tulunid administration – to collect *and* remit revenue collected in the form of both cash and goods. The potential for abuse in such a system is obvious: contractors had every opportunity to exploit the Egyptian populace. The gain was two-fold. The tax contractor enriched himself, all while meeting the terms of the contract and, by extension, securing relations with the state. The story of Ibn Dashuma's interview has the governor address abuses of this kind but, again, its aim is to comment on the quality of Ibn Tulun's leadership.

There is reason, in sum, to challenge this image of the right-minded governor. One way to complicate the picture is to refer again to Ibn Tulun's "pacification campaign": if, as it seems, resistance to oppressive taxation was the main driver of the rebellions, then logic suggests that Ibn Tulun, in crushing the rebels, was better placed than ever to sustain a rigorous tax regime on the Egyptian populace. But the main point, again, concerns the pursuit of authority on Ibn Tulun's part. The biographies, to be fair, are not blind to Ibn Tulun's political savvy: he knew to use the fiscal resources at his disposal to sustain his political program. It is here that we should put our emphasis. The suppression of local opposition and the achievement of authority over the fiscal administration were essential steps in achieving these aims.

There is reason to think that Ibn Tulun took a further step as well, which was to align these aims with the interests of local landholders and merchants. Frantz-Murphy, questioning the image of Ibn Tulun as reformer, argues that his approach probably had more to do with the interests of an emergent Egyptian landed elite working in alliance with the Tulunid house. The wealth of landowning officials derived from two sources: the revenue of their own holdings and the income of high-level positions in the fiscal administration. In most cases, as just seen, appointments of this kind involved tax contracts. They allowed the office holders opportunity to protect the sources of (their own) private wealth and, through their respective offices, see to "the efficient management of the agrarian base of the economy." Ibn Tulun, it seems, served both sets of needs. This, as Frantz-Murphy argues, is an effective way in which to read the accounts of Ibn Tulun's so-called reforms.

The argument connects Ibn Tulun's fiscal and political aims. The *amir* governed with an eye to promoting the interests of his allies, all of whom were heavily invested in the Egyptian economy. As one kind of evidence of elite private holdings, Ibn Tulun is reported to have confiscated estates in Egypt belonging to three opponents: Shuqayr, the former head of the *barid*; Musa ibn Bugha, following the latter's demise; and Ibn al-Mudabbir. Another kind of reference concerns Ibn al-Daya and his father, Yusuf ibn Ibrahim. In a second of his writings, *Al-Mukafa'a*, Ibn al-Daya refers to his own family's landholdings in Egypt, which appear to have been substantial. There is also the reference, voiced by Ibn Tulun in his final testament to Khumarawayh, to the private holdings of the Tulunid house itself.

Assured a firm grip on Egypt's wealth, Ibn Tulun was positioned to take the essential step. It saw him address relations with the Abbasid center. The point has been made already that Ibn Tulun never sought to sever relations with the imperial center. There is every indication, in fact, that he worked hard to nurture these ties with an eye to securing the prestige that accrued from close ties to the Abbasid throne. His aim, rather, was to dictate the terms by which these relations were conducted. Control of Egypt's wealth was the critical ingredient.

His new approach can be seen in his handling of tribute: two references indicate that Ibn Tulun continued to submit payments to the imperial center. Al-Ya'qubi who, again, appears to have worked as a Tulunid finance official, reports that Ibn Tulun sent a sum of 2,100,000 *dirhams*, along with a shipment of *tiraz* and other goods, in 871–872. Al-Balawi, for his part, has Ibn Tulun transfer 1,200,000 *dinars* to Iraq in 875–876. These dates sit well with the timeline of Ibn Tulun's consolidation of control over the Egyptian economy. But Ibn Tulun held office in Egypt for sixteen years and, on this basis, it might be argued that, in submitting large payments only twice, he in fact sought greater independence than is allowed for here.

But these were not the only sums that Ibn Tulun directed to the imperial center. The biographies refer to further instances in which the governor sent revenue to Samarra. These included payments to Tayfur al-Turki and other clients in Iraq. Rather than tribute, these were probably closer to gifts and bribes. More telling still were the sums that Ibn Tulun is reported to have negotiated with al-Mu'-tamid. Ibn al-Daya and al-Balawi describe these as "secret" funds that Ibn Tulun arranged to provide the caliph over a four-year basis, from roughly 875 to 879. The payments clearly suggest an effort to culti-vate political ties in Samarra with the Abbasid court and top military circles. Al-Balawi refers to these payments later as well: in his account of Ibn Tulun's final testimony to Khumarawayh, he has the governor urge his heir to continue delivering the annual sum to the caliph. The passage refers to 100,000 *dinars* annually, describing it as a sacred duty connected directly to the oath of loyalty, the *bay`a*. Ibn Tulun had sworn the oath to God's deputy; this was the symbolic act, carried out in ritual. The payments were the expression of that act.

The "secret payments," it should be said, were not in fact secret. Al-Balawi has al-Muwaffaq complain openly about them. More important still is that Ibn Tulun, in negotiating the arrangement, was imposing conditions on the use of Egyptian revenue. These had partly to do with the confrontation with al-Muwaffaq and the latter's strug-gle to fund the Zanj war. Ibn Tulun did not ignore al-Muwaffaq's need for funding: in 875, as seen earlier, he sent him a payment (the size of which set the regent to grumbling aloud). But Ibn Tulun's ability to withstand the regent's demands, when he saw fit, goes to a larger aim: the governor, Egypt's wealth as his instrument, sought to bend rela-tions with Samarra to his own purposes. This is the main takeaway. Ibn Tulun, using a variety of means, effectively denied the Abbasid state a monopoly over Egypt's revenue. This did not, of course, solve the political questions that he confronted in governing Egypt, sustaining authority in Syria, and confronting Abbasid hostility. But he now had the means by which to tackle them head-on.

CITY AND CEREMONY

Ibn Tulun used Egypt's revenue to shape new-style relations with the Abbasid state. We want to consider his use of that wealth in greater detail. Near Eastern rulers, well before the Islamic era, had known to rely on monument building and public ceremony in staking out political claims. Ibn Tulun followed their lead with the construction of al-Qata'i` and a repertoire of public acts staged against the new urban backdrop. Such measures required considerable expenditure.

Work on al-Qata'i` began in 870, roughly two years after Ibn Tulun's arrival in Egypt. Each of the major venues in the new center had its purpose. Ibn Tulun used the plaza of al-Qata'i`, for example, to stage public ceremonies for his armed forces. Each of the military ceremonies was a projection of strength; Ibn Tulun sought, on the one hand, closer ties to his military command, and on the other, a clear signal to the Egyptian public of the physical might at his disposal. As for the elegant mosque, it served the governor's very public turn to religion, an age-old instrument of Near Eastern politics. A highly visible structure, it provided ample evidence of its patron's commitment to the faith.

Each venue also had its audience. The effort to appeal to a broad public seems clear, but elite audiences led the list: Ibn Tulun was principally concerned with the support of the military command, religious leaders, merchants, and wealthy landholders. The aim was to secure legitimation. Was Ibn Tulun successful in this regard? The record is mixed. His opponents dismissed his efforts. This is evident in Muhammad ibn Da'ud's repeated poetic jabs, the bitter exchanges with al-Muwaffaq and, in its way, the clash with Bakkar ibn Qutayba.

The responses from the Abbasid court are readily explained: Ibn Tulun, in seeking to govern a major province on his own terms, challenged imperial supremacy and the integrity of the empire. Al-Muwaffaq and Ibn Da'ud, in this sense, worked in tandem. Bakkar, as head of the local religious establishment, posed a different sort of challenge, as will be discussed below. There is, however, much to suggest that Ibn Tulun, despite such opposition, succeeded in shaping close working relations with elite Egyptian society.

What of the wider Egyptian public? Ibn al-Daya and al-Balawi make much of Ibn Tulun's devotion to the needs of the Egyptian populace. Anecdotes make the point in different ways. There is the description of the outpouring of grief that followed Ibn Tulun's death in 884: Egyptians – women and men, Jews, Copts, and Muslims – wept in unison at the passing of the great man. These references can be read as an obvious attempt to represent the governor in the best possible light, much in the way of other indications of Ibn Tulun's charity and solic-itude. Such stories, in any case, cannot be corroborated and, indeed, we cannot really know what ordinary Egyptians thought of Ibn Tulun. More to the point is that Ibn Tulun, in all likelihood, was more con-cerned with social order. Such, in any case, is the best way in which to understand his frequent recourse to intimidation and violence. He was quick to remind Egyptians that neither he nor his administration was to be crossed: his subjects were to behave precisely so, as subjects.

AL-QATA'I`

Having resided initially in al-Askar – the first Abbasid headquarters in Egypt, and itself an extension of al-Fustat, the original Arab-Islamic center – the *amir* broke ground on his new administrative and military hub in 870, some two years into his tenure. Again, in doing so, Ibn Tulun tapped into a long Near Eastern tradition of city building, as embodied in the great Sasanid and Byzantine capitals, not to mention the more immediate Abbasid examples of Baghdad and Samarra. A further and more relevant example perhaps was that of al-Abbasiyya, the Aghlabid center outside Qayrawan in Ifriqiya. The Aghlabids, even before Ibn Tulun's arrival in Egypt, had established an autonomous dynasty in North Africa. Their use of urban spaces in projecting a new-style authority may well have impressed Ibn Tulun. Samarra, however, seems certainly to have been his chief source of inspiration.

In constructing al-Qata'i`, Ibn Tulun required the allocation of considerable revenue, the mobilization of a substantial workforce, and the resettlement of a large military and civilian populace. How is it that the *amir* organized a multivalent project of this kind? It bespeaks the presence of an experienced cadre of bureaucrats, builders, artisans, and advisors; the sources, unfortunately, provide little information regarding the minutiae of decision-making and personnel involved in creating the site. It is particularly unfortunate that the sources say only so much about the influence of Samarran patterns on Ibn Tulun and his circle. Given that he was a child of that city, it seems unremarkable that he looked to its example. But was it a matter of nostalgia or an effort to connect his new center to the symbols of imperial might? And did he bring workers and designers from Samarra? The sources tell us too little.

They do provide, however, valuable indications as to Ibn Tulun's ceremonial use of the new space. The initial core elements of al-Qata'i` were a new palace (Ar., *qasr*); a large plaza (Ar., *maydan*); a set of large-scale gates that enclosed the palace-plaza complex; and a main thoroughfare. Al-Maqrizi indicates that Ibn Tulun assigned each of the new city gates a name, elite guard, and specific ceremonial purpose. The largest of the gates stood astride the main avenue. This was the Gate of Prayer (Ar., *Bab al-Salah*), known also as the Gate of Lions (Ar., *Bab al-Siba*), for two prominent plaster lions located to either side of the gate. (While al-Balawi refers to the Gate of Prayer as still extant in his lifetime, it may be, of course, that he is quoting Ibn al-Daya, which would backdate the reference some decades.) The structure itself was composed of three contiguous openings; during ceremonies, the center opening was reserved for the *amir*.

The large mosque and a hospital followed some two years later. Al-Balawi hails both projects as evidence of the *amir*'s determination to carry out pious works. Built of baked brick on a quadrilateral plan, and enclosed by high walls, the mosque is an early example of the congregational style in Islamic sacred architecture. Its exterior walls, on three sides, are separated from those of the mosque proper by wide spaces known as *ziyadat* (Ar., sing. *ziyada*), a stylistic feature borrowed from Samarran mosques. Its large open courtyard is surrounded by wide arcades: a set of two parallel arcades on each of three sides and a set of five arcades on the fourth side in which was located the *mihrab*, the wall niche that marks the direction of prayer (Ar., *qibla*). The large fountain that visitors to the mosque see today probably dates to the thirteenth-century reign of the Mamluk sultan, Husam al-Din Lajin. The original is said to have been an elaborate structure crowned with a dome. It is reported to have been the site where the call to prayer (Ar., *idhan*) was issued in the Tulunid period.

Heavy piers, rather than pillars, support the arches that make up the arcades; the undersides of the arches – the soffits – contain fine geometric and floral stucco carvings, also a feature of Abbasid mosques. An anecdote explains the absence of pillars. It has Ibn Tulun accept advice from a Christian architect, a mysterious figure described in the sources as a "Christian" (Ar., *nasrani*), not a Copt (Ar., *qibt*), indicating perhaps that he was of non-Egyptian origin. Recruited by Ibn Tulun to construct an aqueduct, he was then imprisoned for a misdeed. Seconding Ibn Tulun's concern that the use of columns in the mosque would have required looting local churches and smaller mosques – an irreligious act that the *amir* opposed – the architect won his freedom. More to the point, he also won the commission to build the mosque, again by pushing the use of the brick piers.

The mosque was joined by two further structures: a secondary palace (Ar., *Dar al-Imara*) and the famous spiral minaret. Al-Maqrizi, writing centuries later, speaks of the ceremonies that accompanied Ibn Tulun's use of the first of these structures (his description is treated below). In attaching the small residence to his mosque, Ibn Tulun was following a well-established imperial pattern evident not only in Samarra, for example, with the mosque of Abu Dulaf, but in much earlier structures from the Umayyad period on. As for the minaret, it appears that the original Tulunid tower was replaced in the thirteenth century; the original structure is thought to have more clearly resembled the spiral form found in Samarra in the minarets of al-Mutawakkil and, again, Abu Dulaf. All three minarets boasted a wide exterior staircase, a feature of early Islamic-Near Eastern construction.

On completion of the mosque, Ibn Tulun ordered up what seems to have been at least two copies of a long foundation inscription. Carved in the Kufic style of inscriptional Arabic, the marble plaques were likely placed facing out onto the central courtyard. Only large fragments of the inscription survive, so it is impossible to establish the full text of each inscription and the actual number of copies produced. There is also the question of where Ibn Tulun intended to display the other copies of the plaques. The inscription joined Ibn Tulun's name and title to a set of Qur'anic verses. These speak, in part, of earthly and divine reward for righteous deeds, notably the raising of "houses of God" (Q. 24:36–37), typically interpreted to mean mosques and other venues of worship. It was a stark visual reminder to worshippers – the Muslim populace of Egypt – of Ibn Tulun's standing as both founder and patron. The reference reads: "The *amir*, Abu al-Abbas Ahmad ibn Tulun, client of the Commander of the Faithful." The latter title, of course, belonged to the caliph, in this case, al-Mu'tamid; the phrase recalls the placement of Ibn Tulun's name alongside that of the caliph on Tulunid coinage.

Al-Maqrizi writes that contemporaries were struck by the grandeur of the new mosque; other medieval writers, including travelers, wrote of its impressive appearance. The sources also speak of popular stories that sprang up following its construction. So, for example, Ibn Tulun was advised – by "the righteous people" (Ar., *salihun*) who had long worshipped at the site – to locate the mosque on Jabal Yashkur, a rocky high point in the middle of al-Qata'i`. Popular lore assigned the site an impressive religious past: it was there that Abraham carried out his sacrifice and Moses entreated God. It was also on Jabal Yashkur that individuals of particular renown in (Islamic) Egyptian history had either worshipped or been interred. The list includes Fatima al-Zahra, the Prophet's daughter, and Harun (Aaron), which refers either to the biblical (and Qur'anic) prophet or the Prophet Muhammad's great-grandson, Harun ibn Husayn ibn Ali. It is simple guesswork whether such associations were shaped in the Tulunid or in later periods.

But no less striking are stories that point to the mosque as controversial, in this case concerning the revenue used to pay for its construction. The foundation inscription includes wording that the revenue derived from a "pure and licit source." This was, admittedly, stock language that appears in many inscriptions on mosques and other structures from the first centuries of Islam. The phrasing connects with a Qur'anic principle (Q. 59:6–7) that seems to indicate that wealth granted by God to the Prophet and, by extension, any Muslim leader, was properly dedicated to social and religious needs (e.g., support for the needy). The idea was that the patron of the new site – Ibn Tulun – could vouch for the "purity" of the revenue in question.

The stories, from two later Egyptian sources, concern complaints voiced against Ibn Tulun's project. Ibn Duqmaq (d. c. 1406), a fourteenth-century scholar, has local Muslims confront the governor: "We do not know the origins of the money that [you] used to build it." Ibn Iyas (fl. early sixteenth century), another later author, has local Muslims refuse to worship in the mosque on grounds that, "it was built with tainted money and thus it is not permissible to pray there." The texts have Ibn Tulun respond in a Friday sermon – one example of his use of religiously-charged spaces – in which he insisted that he had paid for the construction using only income of divine providence.

The reference is to the famous episode – touched on earlier – in which Ibn Tulun chanced upon a buried treasure, either in the desert or on Muqattam, the small mountain overlooking al-Fustat. The accounts have him devote the sums to pious works including the hospital, stipends for scholars, and the mosque itself. It was, Ibn Tulun argued, divine compensation for his righteous conduct. Ibn Iyas's account, as if to underscore the point, adds a dream sequence in which the Prophet himself inspires the *amir* with ideas on designing the mosque. These accounts, read critically, had likely to do with debates dating to the lifetimes of the two authors, that is, the later Mamluk period. But they may also echo arguments surrounding Ibn Tulun's rise to prominence: the new building, a prominent feature of the Egyptian landscape, was a suitable topic for debates of this kind.

The second of the two projects, the hospital (Ar., *bimaristan*), may have been located in fact in al-Askar. Al-Qalqashandi (d. 1418), also a Mamluk-era scholar, refers to the structure as extant in his lifetime. Nothing remains, it seems, of the building today. Ibn Tulun, evidently much attached to the project, directed that income from commercial properties and, interestingly, the slave market in al-Fustat, be used to provide for patients, medicines, and a trained staff.

Few traces, sadly, remain of al-Qata'i`, unlike, say, the ruin fields of Abbasid Samarra. There is evidence that the main palace survived into the early Fatimid period, and, as just noted, Ibn Tulun's hospital into the Mamluk period. Apart, however, from the grand mosque and a small section of Ibn Tulun's aqueduct, only fragmentary remains of two Tulunid-era residences and a bath (Ar., *hammam*), discovered in 1933 in the area of al-Askar, have survived to the present day. The sources indicate that much of al-Qata'i` was destroyed during the Abbasid assault in 905. The building of Cairo in the late tenth century probably erased whatever else remained.

THE CITY AS STAGE

Ibn Tulun is reported to have broken ground on al-Qata'i` directly after his return from the aborted campaign against Ibn al-Shaykh in 870. The sources connect it to the expansion of the Tulunid military. Al-Maqrizi, speaking of al-Askar, puts it this way: "It reached the point that because of the press of the [newly acquired] slave [troops], the infantry, and the stores of materiel, space in the [old] palace grounds grew constricted and there was no longer any way in which to further expand [it]." Ibn Tulun, faced with rising complaints, selected a site on the Muqattam plateau, northwest of al-Fustat. The site is described as having been occupied by Jewish and Christian tombs; Ibn Tulun had them removed to make way for the new center. It is a plausible account: overcrowding is a reason to expand, and the governor's effort to accommodate his armed forces has been noted. But it is clear that Ibn Tulun had much else in mind as well for what amounted to a new capital.

There is, first of all, the strong likelihood that Ibn Tulun sought to attach al-Qata'i` to the legacy of the great imperial centers and, specifically, that of the Abbasid house. Al-Qata'i`, visually speaking, "quoted" directly from Samarra and, by extension, Baghdad. Many of the shared features may have been routine elements of Arab-Islamic imperial construction. But the range and number of parallels suggests a deliberate effort. Again, it is unfortunate that so little information exists regarding the artisans and workers involved in constructing al-Qata'i`. The question remains open, in particular, as to whether Ibn Tulun recruited Egyptian (Coptic and Muslim) builders or relied chiefly on imported labor from Iraq and Syria.

The list of parallel features included the monumental gates and walls; the placement of a central avenue; the arrangement of markets by type; the allocation of lots to ethnically designated regiments; animal parks; and gardens devoted to recreation. Activities held on the *Maydan* probably included equestrian sports, all reminiscent of the polo grounds and racecourses of the Iraqi imperial cities. There is also the look of the minaret and the use of *ziyadat*, both of which speak to a Samarran inspiration. Further parallels include the use of baked, red brick; the application of plaster to the brick surfaces; and the inclusion of fine woodcarvings (in Ibn Tulun's mosque, the carving appears most dramatically in a frieze containing Qur'anic inscriptions, sections of which can still be seen today). Stuccowork, in the mosque and the ruins in al-Askar, bear a clear Samarran stamp, specifically in the use of floral and other natural motifs.

Descriptions provided by al-Ya`qubi of the founding of Baghdad and, some seventy years later, Samarra, indicate that the caliphs al-Mansur and al-Mu`tasim attended closely to the layout and construction of their respective capitals. Like al-Qata'i`, the two imperial centers began as state projects. Each city was an emblem of power, a physical expression of the pre-eminence and piety of its respective builder.

Working in tandem with the many visual reminders were also a set of functional elements. Thus, for example, al-Qata'i` provided Ibn Tulun and his court the means by which to strengthen relations with elite civilians and military officers. This goes to the lands that Ibn Tulun distributed to members of both circles. As al-Balawi puts it, Ibn Tulun "directed his elite companions, slave clients and followers to settle themselves around him; they selected lots and built upon them such that the developed area reached the boundary of al-Fustat." The landed properties, as gestures of patronage, came with significant expectations of loyalty and service attached. In this sense, al-Qata'i` acted as the venue of social mobility for both newly ascendant elites and their patron, Ibn Tulun. Such are the means by which elite networks were sustained.

The properties were also a source of wealth and, thus, local prestige. The recipients of the land grants, with the demand that they build upon them, were expected to produce income, in the form of rents, commercial profits, and other revenue. An open question is whether such revenue was to go to the Tulunid treasury and then redistributed in the form of salaries, stipends, and other expenditures, or if the new landholders retained some measure of the revenue directly. Related here, as well, are the markets in al-Qata'i`: it would seem likely, given Ibn Tulun's relations with the landholding elite of Egypt, that he provided full access, perhaps even control, of the markets to these circles. But here, too, we have to guess as to how such fiscal arrangements were structured.

And, finally, Ibn Tulun, as commander-in-chief, also used the new center to accommodate his new regiments. This involved the provision of housing. But there is reason to think that the settlement policy also provided the governor and his military command with the means by which to impose discipline on the rank and file. There is a suggestion in the following passage that the barracks of al-Qata'i` were closely ordered.

> The different lots were divided up, each named after those who settled on it. So the African troops (Ar., *Nuba*) had a distinct property named after them, the Greek-speaking units (Ar., *Rum*) had a distinct property named after them, the auxiliary units (Ar., *farrashun*) had a distinct property named after them, and to every [other] category of slave troops (Ar., *ghilman*) a distinct property named after them. Their officers saw to construction on a number of sites.

It bears repeating that the policy of military settlement was much like that used in Baghdad and Samarra. As in both imperial cities, units were settled according to ethnic and/or geographic origin and placed under the command of key officers.

The new city must have left a strong visual impression. This can only have been enhanced by its regular use as a ceremonial center. Al-Qata'i`, like Baghdad and Samarra, its imperial counterparts, functioned as a public stage. Ibn Tulun, the product of a military household and, for much of his formative life, a denizen of Samarra, probably needed little reminder of the value of formal ceremony. The sources have Ibn Tulun preside over a variety of public activities of this kind. In at least some cases, these were intended to address several audiences at once.

So, for example, in presiding over ceremonies on feast days – a likely reference to the two canonical festivals of the Muslim year, the *Id al-Adha* and the *Id al-Fitr* – Ibn Tulun was flanked by elite troops, a reminder to all of the force at his disposal. The sources refer, alongside the major feast days, to two additional occasions on the Tulunid calendar: the "day of almsgiving" (Ar., *yawm al-sadaqat*) – or, alternatively, the "day of the poor" (Ar., *masakin*) – and the "day of military review" (Ar., *yawm al-ard*). It remains unclear if these were formal occasions, observed each calendar year, or more episodic. The day of almsgiving, in any case, entailed the use of feeding stations at which bread and meats were distributed to the needy. The military review presumably involved the formal assembly of troops, equipment, and mounts.

As these references suggest, Ibn Tulun assigned uses to the different spaces of al-Qata'i`: he knew to use the public arena to good effect. A further example concerns the gates that led into the main plaza, and which were assigned specific functions. These were normally accessed on a fixed schedule but, on feast days, were opened for general use. Regarding the hospital, al-Balawi reports that Ibn Tulun arranged to have a pair of physicians provide care to indigent patients each Friday and saw to the provision of expensive medicines: "[these] were normally only found in the supply stores of kings and caliphs." The *amir* is said to have carried out regular inspections of patients and grounds, suggesting, of course, an understanding of the political rewards of being seen. To this end, perhaps, he is said to have ordered that care at the hospital be provided only to civilians; troops and slaves were kept away. He also ordered a physician to be on hand at the mosque, "should anything befall the worshippers during prayer." Ibn Tulun thus did his part in promoting the medical sciences, a dynamic field in the Abbasid period. The hospital's presence and function speak to the flourishing of regional centers of Islamic culture and scholarship by the ninth century.

But here, as elsewhere, Ibn Tulun could not avoid controversy. Muhammad ibn Da'ud – the poet thorn beneath Ibn Tulun's saddle – referenced the hospital in one of several compositions that al-Kindi included in his chronicle. The poet, whose touch was seldom subtle, describes Ibn Tulun as "an affliction" visited upon the unsuspecting people of Egypt, an untutored and small-minded "roughneck" (Ar., *ilj*); he may have provided for the sick but also assaulted their women. Ibn Da'ud closes the poem with the accusation, noted earlier, that the governor, secure behind his ceremonial curtain, turned a deaf ear to the entreaties of his subjects. The poet manages to dismiss governor and Egypt's citizens alike, the latter for pinning their hopes on Ibn Tulun. One would like to know not only more of Ibn Da'ud's sentiments but also why al-Kindi, a son of Egypt, included the verse in his account of the governor's career. The indications – that not all Egyptians thought well of Ibn Tulun – are evident.

The principal palace of al-Qata'i᷾ served as a ceremonial venue in no less a fashion. The sources provide little sense of the dimensions and appearance of the palace. They do refer, however, to Ibn Tulun's frequent turn to *mazalim* sessions, which likely took place in the palace. A well-established practice by the late ninth century, these were judicial sessions in which members of the public brought grievances to a ruler to be resolved. These claims typically had to do with illicit acts of injustice or corruption by state officials. It is this practice on Ibn Tulun's part that is referred to in the story of Umm Uqba, although the story does not use the term (*mazalim*) directly. The story acts as reminder to readers that here, as elsewhere, Ibn Tulun behaved properly.

There are also references to a second ceremonial practice that attached to the palace. This concerned what might be called Ibn Tulun's "viewing rooms" (Ar., *majlis*, pl. *majalis*). Open-air spaces, it seems, and furnished to accommodate the governor and elite guests, these were used by Ibn Tulun to preside over a variety of proceedings. The governor is said to have had two such spaces constructed, one atop the main palace, from which he could observe activity in the grand plaza, the other on the Gate of Prayer overlooking al-Qata'i''s main avenue. He appears to have used the space atop the palace for the Days of Almsgiving and Review, the other space on feast days. Al-Maqrizi, citing Muhammad al-Quda'i (d. 1062), a prominent Fatimid-era scholar, refers to the "belvedere" (Ar., *manzar*) constructed by Ibn Tulun for the "cavalry review" (Ar., *ard al-khayl*; probably corresponding with the Day of Military Review), as one of the "four wonders of Islam," but which, at some point, fell out of use.

The use of the viewing spaces appears to have been yet a further borrowing from Abbasid practice: the Bab al-Amma, a three-part monumental gate and thus prominent feature of al-Mu'tasim's palace complex at Samarra, is thought to have contained a second-floor *majlis* as did the palace in al-Mansur's Round City at Baghdad. Seated in the *majlis*, and presumably visible to all onlookers, Ibn Tulun is described as having missed nothing. So, for example, on review days, Ibn Tulun, noting that a given guardsman (Ar., *ghulam*) was deficient in appearance, would order the provision of the missing gear. A second anecdote has Ibn Tulun note the distress of an elderly beggar, caught up in the throngs seeking food; he orders the man to be provided with immediate assistance. The anecdotes speak to the notion of the "all-seeing" prince as well as Ibn Tulun's appetite for justice.

Ibn Tulun made his presence felt, as well, in exploiting the physical and symbolic power of the mosque. The *Dar al-Imara*, the smaller of Ibn Tulun's two residences, abutted the mosque's *qibla* wall. It was designed, in part, to give access to the mosque itself through a doorway that opened directly into the *maqsura* (the space, located at the front of the mosque near the *mihrab*, that was set off from the main prayer hall for the ruler and his household). In al-Maqrizi's description, Ibn Tulun proceeded each Friday from the principal palace down the main thoroughfare, through the Gate of Prayer, and into the small residence. Suggested, of course, is a dignified procession with onlookers lined up along the way; it seems right to assume, as well, given Ibn Tulun's frequent turn to intimidation, that many onlookers felt it prudent to take part in what appears to have been a weekly ritual. The *amir*, having repeated his ablutions and changed into appropriate dress for the Friday prayer, then proceeded into the mosque and, thus, into public view.

THE MILITARY COMMAND

Al-Qata'i' provided Ibn Tulun with the means by which to see and be seen. Processions, public feast days, and Friday prayer sessions: each had its ceremonial function. And the governor, in having his new center echo the Abbasid cities, sought to associate himself with well-understood trappings of power. He also knew to speak to specific audiences. Al-Ya'qubi, in his chronicle, refers twice to Ibn Tulun in his brief description of events in the year 872. This was approximately four years into the governor's tenure in office, and two years after his campaign against Ibn al-Shaykh and the creation of the new Egypt-based slave military units. The one reference appears to describe an elaborate ceremony.

> In this year, Ahmad ibn Tulun took the oath of allegiance to himself from the army, the *shakiriyya*, the freedmen, and elite circles (*al-nas*): they were to treat as enemies all whom he saw as enemies, treat as allies all whom he saw as allies, and wage war against all whom he waged war.

Two elusive terms occur here. A reasonable translation of *shakiriyya* is "palace guard," indicating that these were troops tasked especially with the protection of the governor, his family, and elite society. The term, probably of Central Asian derivation, occurs in references to elements of the ninth-century Abbasid military. These may have been units that accompanied Ibn Tulun to Egypt; in any case, it is further indication of the complex makeup of the Tulunid armed forces. The second term is *al-nas*, which typically denotes "[the] people," although, in many contexts, it can mean elite circles, so perhaps, here, it refers to the military command and Ibn Tulun's top civilian supporters. The passage serves the point that Ibn Tulun devoted himself to securing the loyalties of his military.

The second event concerned what al-Ya'qubi refers to as the "Talibids." The term denotes the descendants of the family of Ali ibn Abi Talib and Fatima, the son-in-law and daughter of the Prophet Muhammad. As members of the Prophet's House, these individuals were accorded particular deference in Islamic society. On a number of occasions in the early Islamic period, family members led rebellions and other acts of opposition to Umayyad and Abbasid rule. Several opponents of Abbasid rule in Egypt are identified as Alids (followers of the Prophet's family), including Ibn al-Arqat, Ibn Tabataba, and Ibn al-Sufi, all of whose efforts were subdued by Tulunid forces.

The brief passage from al-Ya'qubi refers to measures taken by Ibn Tulun against an otherwise unidentified group of Talibids and the punishment of one such person. The measures included torture and public shaming.

> In this year, Ahmad ibn Tulun sent the Talibids from Egypt to Medina with an escort. Their departure took place in Jumada al-Thani [April 872]. One of the descendants of al-Abbas ibn Ali [ibn Abi Talib] remained, intending instead to make for North Africa. Ahmad ibn Tulun had him arrested, whipped 150 strokes and paraded in public around al-Fustat.

The two events in 872 – the ceremony of oath-taking by the military and the crackdown on the Talibids – can be treated together. Each public act was a show of strength and each involved the military; the second event, the exile of the Talibids, had Ibn Tulun rely on his security forces to execute a politically sensitive decision, including the harsh beating of the one unnamed individual. In this way Ibn Tulun addressed twin goals: closer relations with his commanders and a firm stance against a potent source of religious and political opposition. The second element had Ibn Tulun play a significant religious card. His turn to religion for political aims is discussed further on. Here the topic is his relationship with the military.

The ceremony of oath-taking was only one of many events that Ibn Tulun organized for the armed forces, and his military command in particular. The events included appointments by Ibn Tulun during his second Syria campaign, that which followed the death of Amajur in 877. Ibn Tulun, in each of several Syrian cities, appointed as resident governors either his own men or individuals that had previously served Amajur. Each appointment likely involved a public ceremony. The examples of Muhammad ibn Rafi and Ahmad ibn Da'bash – both men had served Amajur – were cited earlier.

The sources provide better information on ceremonies that Ibn Tulun organized in Egypt proper, including the two events referred to by al-Ya'qubi. These combined several ingredients: a victory declaration; the display and/or public punishment of vanquished opponents; and gestures honoring the commanders. Each ingredient can be seen in the campaigns of pacification carried out – against Ibn al-Arqat, Ibn Tabataba, Ibn al-Sufi, al-Umari, Abu Ruh Sukun, and the rebels of Barka – in the first years of Ibn Tulun's tenure. One thinks, as well, of the triumph over al-Abbas in 879–880.

The best example of a victory announcement comes in reference to Ibn al-Arqat: the rebel leader, an Alid, was sent to Iraq with a Tulunid letter announcing delivery of the prisoner and the hard-won victory over the rebellion. It can be reasonably assumed that Ibn Tulun circulated documents following the other campaigns as well. As for the public treatment of opponents, this took various forms. Most often – as in the case of the unnamed Talibid punished for seeking entry to North Africa or the followers of Ibn al-Arqat – it was a matter of ritualized violence, notably beheadings and the display of physical remains.

The rituals organized for each commander, the third ingredient, is also clear. Al-Balawi briefly describes the triumph over Ibn Tabataba. The rebel appeared near Barqa then in the Egyptian interior, suggesting that his following was mobile and rural. That he appealed to his followers on religious grounds is suggested by the reference to him as an Alawi. To contain the revolt, Ibn Tulun sent Buhm ibn al-Husayn; the commander returned to al-Fustat with the rebel's head. The assumption is that, upon his entry to al-Qata'i', Buhm presented the grim trophy to Ibn Tulun and received an appropriate reward. Al-Balawi provides better detail in regard to Ibn al-Sufi. Following reports that the latter's followers had ransacked Asna, Ibn Tulun sent units under Ibn Yazdad. Ibn al-Sufi, following his defeat of Ibn Yazdad, ordered the display of his dismembered body. Such practice was customary, a grisly act carried out by state actors and opponents alike. Ibn Tulun responded with a second force led by Buhm. The latter, near the town of Akhmim, routed Ibn al-Sufi's forces; the passage refers to the slaughter of a "large number" of his followers. Ibn al-Sufi himself escaped. The text then describes Buhm's entry to al-Fustat.

> Buhm ibn al-Husayn, on his return, informed Ibn Tulun of what had transpired. Ibn Tulun bestowed on him honorary robes and an elaborate belt of burnished gold. He also presented him with a number of fine horses. Buhm, when riding in procession on feast days, was always sure to display the belt.

Evidence drawn from Central Asia suggests that the bestowal and display of fine belts was an established practice there and in eastern Iran, and subsequently used in Abbasid military circles until at least the tenth century. Ibn Tulun's repeated turn to the practice, in strengthening ties to his commanders, suggests that it flourished in Samarra.

The ingredients – celebration of victory, the display of physical remains, and the honors bestowed on commanders – appear in descriptions of the other campaigns as well. So, for example, Ibn Tulun staged a public ceremony to honor al-Umari that featured the ritual burial of the rebel's head and the execution of his assassins. As for the campaign against Abu Ruh Sukun, Ibn Tulun is described as having collaborated closely with his commanders in bringing it to a successful end. Here, too, ritual violence played a part: the governor ordered the bodies of two of the rebel's supporters to be suspended from a bridge over the Nile. As for the rebellion at Barqa, Ibn Tulun worked closely with Lu'lu', his long-time client turned field commander. Lu'lu' is described as having entered the defeated city after a long siege. After executing a number of the rebel leaders, and placing their bodies on display, he wrote to Ibn Tulun with a victory announcement. Al-Balawi describes his triumphant return to Egypt.

> Lu'lu' entered al-Fustat with a large number of captives in tow, and whose fate he placed in the hands of his master. Ibn Tulun, at Giza, presented him with a fine robe and two thick and finely wrought belts. Wearing the robe and belts, and with the captives on display, Lu'lu' processed through the city.

The passage ends with a comment on the response of Egyptians to Ibn Tulun's ever-stronger hand: "a new trepidation filled their hearts."

This view of the governor can hardly have changed when, some five years on, in 879–880, Ibn Tulun marked the collapse of al-Abbas's rebellion with a ceremony that featured all three ingredients. The victory announcement came in a letter from al-Wasiti, Ibn Tulun's long-time advisor. The letter, in all likelihood, was read aloud. The element of ritual violence included the display of heads belonging to members of al-Abbas's army and the terrible ceremony in which Ibn Tulun forced his son to execute his companions. The event concluded with a presentation of expensive robes, fine horses, and sacks of coins to Tabarji, the commander in question, and his subordinates. Ibn Tulun had the full army on hand to greet the officers upon their return, prisoners and severed heads on show.

Ibn Tulun made a point, in sum, of securing close relations with his armed forces. The results, however, were mixed. The success of his military build-up seems clear: he created a large, complex force that he himself commanded, with the support of loyal officers. It was an autonomous force, independent of Abbasid imperial command and sustained entirely by the Tulunid treasury. His success in creating an effective military can be seen in the defeats of Ibn al-Arqat and other opponents in Egypt as well as the two Syria campaigns. The sources indicate that Ibn Tulun faced no further opposition in Egypt in the later part of his reign. Ibn Tulun asked much of his armed forces and, in return, compensated them handsomely.

But problems persisted. There are indications of discipline problems among the Tulunid rank and file, for example and, on two occasions, Tulunid forces withdrew from Tarsus in lieu of imposing local control. The first episode, it is true, involved a tactical decision on Ibn Tulun's part; on the second occasion, however, the forces of Tarsus held off Ibn Tulun's army and finally forced its withdrawal. The defection of Lu'lu' can be mentioned as well: it deprived Ibn Tulun not only of an experienced field commander but the units under his authority as well. Finally, we have the routing in 883 of a Tulunid force in Mecca. The episode is obscure. Ibn Tulun is reported to have sent a mixed force of cavalry and foot soldiers with a large sum of money to be distributed to the Meccan populace. The local Abbasid garrison, supported by troops sent from Samarra, drove off the Tulunid units. The episode occurred during the Hajj and, according to al-Balawi, was connected to Ibn Tulun's confrontation with al-Muwaffaq. Again, difficult to explain, the episode does suggest at least that the Tulunid military became overstretched.

THE RELIGIOUS ESTABLISHMENT

Ibn Tulun's turn to religion – his reliance on Islamic symbolism and rhetoric – is hardly surprising. Religion suffused Abbasid political life, as it had Near Eastern cultures for centuries; all political actors, and especially new claimants to authority, had little option but to seek legitimation on these grounds. The effort offered no guarantees but, without it, there was little sense in trying.

The context in Ibn Tulun's case was the slow Islamization of Egypt. Modern scholars have long debated the emergence of a Muslim majority in the Nile Valley. This meant, in good part, the conversion of Egypt's Jews and Coptic Christians. One view dates the tipping point to the late ninth-early tenth century, another view to the fourteenth century. That the dating varies so widely speaks to the scarcity of good information. What seems certain, in any case, is that Ibn Tulun governed an increasingly complex Muslim population: the descendants of the first Arab-Muslim conquerors, generations of eighth and ninth-century Muslim immigrants to Egypt, and the convert populace itself.

There is comparatively little information on Ibn Tulun's relations with Egypt's non-Muslim communities. One report has the Jewish inhabitants of al-Fustat join with Christians and Muslims in a massive rally, organized by the dying governor himself, in which the faithful appealed for his divine protection. As for the Coptic Church and its majority following, there are but a handful of references, including passing mentions of Christian officials in the Tulunid administration and, as noted earlier, the obscure Christian architect of Ibn Tulun's mosque. *The History of the Patriarchs*, a major Coptic source, describes a controversy late in Ibn Tulun's tenure that led to a confrontation with the Coptic patriarch, Michael (Mikhail) III (880–907). And edited papyrus documents, an invaluable source, make clear that the Tulunid fiscal administration interacted on a consistent basis with local Christian communities, as would be expected. But, otherwise, the extent and dynamics of the interaction between the Tulunid administration and what was still Egypt's largest socio-religious population eludes us.

The sources are mostly interested in Ibn Tulun's approach to Egypt's Muslims. His turn to religion joined several threads. There was, first, the governor's own piety. Was it for show, that is, political gain? His biographers insist it was not: they have him motivated by faith at every turn. They describe him as a *hafiz* (an individual who has committed the entire Qur'an to memory), refer to his deep interest in Hadith, and cite his long training with religious scholars on the Byzantine-Islamic frontier. Reference can also be made to the scholarly career of Adnan, Ibn Tulun's one son, as seen below. It suggests the extent to which the Tulunid household, over three generations, integrated fully into Near Eastern and Islamic culture.

But Ibn Tulun's use of religion in the public arena, for political purposes, can hardly be denied. Later authors echo Ibn al-Daya and al-Balawi in this regard. Ibn al-Athir (d. 1233), a thirteenth-century Iraqi scholar, describes Ibn Tulun as "much given to righteous acts of charity and deep piety; committed to the religious scholars and men of faith; and devoted to deeds of godliness and the interests of Muslims." Muhammad ibn Da'ud's mocking comment, noted previously, tries to spoil the effect: "How great the entreaties [of the people (*al-nas*)] to one behind his curtain/they appeal to a heart neglectful of God." The reference is vague but it likely refers to Ibn Tulun's use of the *mazalim* sessions. These occasions allowed individuals to approach the governor directly and, for Ibn Tulun, a venue for public gestures of faith and pious commitment; the "curtain" refers to the custom of placing monarchs and princes out of view during public sessions, though this is almost the only reference to Ibn Tulun using the practice. The wrinkle, however, was that these sessions were distinct from the courts of Islamic law administered by judges (Ar., *qadis*), that is, members of the Sunni religious elite. Tulunid Egypt, in other words, much like the Abbasid state, witnessed the use of two judicial systems, each charged with the assurance of justice and order, but in separate areas of the law.

One issue, then, in considering Ibn Tulun's turn to Islam, is his relations with the religious establishment. In negotiating such relations he, much like the Abbasids themselves, had to walk a fine line. Easy interaction with jurists, prayer leaders and scholars was by no means assured. The *amir*'s confrontation with Bakkar ibn Qutayba speaks to this dynamic: relations between religious leaders and the Abbasid empire's political and military elite, whether local governors, regional pretenders, or the Abbasid caliphs themselves, were often strained. In Ibn Tulun's case, it was, at its root, a question of boundaries – how far could such a person claim legitimation on religious grounds?

The governor, on a number of occasions, is said to have sought out expressions of support from Muslim elites. These typically involved public gatherings and/or formal declarations. Acts of public charity, as on feast days, were occasions of this kind, and Ibn Tulun evidently organized them on a regular basis. If the references have to do with crafting an *image* of Ibn Tulun as dutiful governor, repeated activity of this kind by Ibn Tulun cannot be ruled out. Another type of occasion speaks to the need for legal sanction specifically. Ibn Tulun, before his time in Egypt, had called on the *qadi* of Wasit and official witnesses to confirm that al-Musta'in was physically sound prior to his execution. As governor, Ibn Tulun is said to assembled witnesses to attest that Shuqayr al-Khadim's corpse bore no signs of obvious ill-treatment; to have summoned witnesses to confirm his formal transfer of tribute to Amajur, the Syrian governor, probably in 875–876; and to have dispatched a delegation of religious notables to al-Abbas in the effort to negotiate an end to the latter's rebellion. Ibn Tulun is also reported to have sent a delegation of scholars and others to Samarra at the moment of his assignment over Egypt's finances.

Ibn Tulun thus interacted regularly with religious leaders. These contacts go to this question of religion as a main source of Ibn Tulun's authority. The context of eighth- and ninth-century Islamic history cannot be treated here in detail, but it bears recalling that the complex process of Islamization, whether in Egypt or elsewhere, involved not simply the conversion of local communities to the new faith. At issue, as well, was the gradual shaping of different currents of Islam. To most historians, the shaping of both the Sunni and (various branches of) Shi`i Islam was in full swing in the late ninth century. Ibn Tulun can be identified as a "Sunni" Muslim, although such a designation would not have been as apparent in late ninth-century Egypt as it is today. More helpful, perhaps, is to speak of the "proto-Sunnism" of the majority Muslim populace of Tulunid Egypt, but with the reminder that references to Alid activity indicates that other Islamic religious currents were present in Egypt as well.

Ibn Tulun's early education in Tarsus points to another piece of the early Islamic puzzle. The frontier scholars contributed to "proto-Sunni" thought and practice; the sources, indicating Ibn Tulun's keen interest in sustaining ties to these circles, suggest his awareness of these ideas. But characteristic of early Sunni Islam as well was the emergence of self-designated "schools" of Islamic law (Ar., *madhhab*, pl. *madhahib*). These sprang from the teachings of prominent urban scholars, whose students, over generations, gave shape, through education, patronage, and self-identification, to distinct legal traditions. By the late ninth-early tenth century, it appears that the *madhahib* also became the locus of social prestige for Muslim scholars and their circles of followers. Religious leaders, secure in their public support, wielded a distinct form of social authority.

Thus, unsurprisingly, rivalries emerged between schools at the local level. Tulunid Egypt is a case in point. There is the matter of Bakkar, in his capacity as head of the judiciary, as will be seen shortly; his confrontation with Ibn Tulun perhaps involved differences in religious affiliation. Mention should also be made of Adnan, a third of Ibn Tulun's sons, whose career route contrasted with that of his brothers, al-Abbas and Khumarawayh, both of whom immersed themselves in the world of palace politics and military life. Ibn Asakir (d. 1176), a twelfth-century Damascene scholar, describes Adnan by contrast as a scholar, immersed in the study of Hadith, the law, and education.

He identifies Adnan specifically as a Shafi`i scholar, thus a member of one of four emergent Sunni legal "schools." The term refers to Muhammad ibn Idris al-Shafi'i (d. 820), a foundational figure in Sunni law (and a resident of Egypt at the end of his life, his tomb a popular visitation site). Ibn Asakir has Adnan sitting in, as a boy, to sessions led by Rabi'a ibn Sulayman al-Muradi, a student of the great master and, for years, a principal proponent of al-Shafi'i's teachings in Egypt. It also refers to confrontations between students of al-Shafi'i and members of the Maliki school, a second of the proto-Sunni legal circles. The Malikis had been predominant in Egypt prior to the spread of the Shafi'i movement. The text has Ibn Tulun, on hearing news of the clashes, direct his men to support the Shafi'is such that the latter gained an upper hand. The governor also ordered payments made to Rabi'a and his family.

Ibn Tulun's intervention in support of the Shafi'is provides reason to identify him as an adherent of the one legal "school." One presumes that it furthered his relations with one of Egypt's elite religious circles as well. But the governor, by taking sides in a factional conflict was, one thinks, laying claim to a religiously infused authority of his own. If the effort was meant to serve his political agenda, it also left him vulnerable to criticism that he had no business making such claims. This is to see elite religious figures as significant public actors: Bakkar seldom shied from holding ground against the governor when he saw fit. The issue came to the foreground at the point of the Damascus Assembly as has been previously described.

There remains a further question regarding Ibn Tulun's turn to religion. A characteristic of proto-Sunni Islam was its distinction, on doctrinal, legal, and ritual grounds, from Shi'ism. Modern scholars typically see Sunni Islam, in fact, as having emerged as a response to the emergence of (the different expressions of) Shi'i Islam. The report from al-Ya'qubi concerning the arrest of the unidentified Talibid may be an indication that Ibn Tulun, consciously or not, contributed to an accelerating sectarian divide within the Islamic realm. The sources provide only hints in this regard: the reference to the exiling of the Talibids but also the clashes with Ibn al-Arqat, Ibn Tabataba, and Ibn al-Sufi, all three of whom are identified as Alid leaders. But, if only hints, they certainly point to a pattern whereby Ibn Tulun sought political advantage in making public his religious affiliations.

DAMASCUS, THE ABBASID COURT, AND THE FRONTIER

The Damascus Assembly in 883 brought together several elements of Ibn Tulun's political experiment. Ending, as it did, with little resolved between him and his opponents, it reminds us that his effort to assert himself on the imperial stage fell short. The event can be summed up in brief. Ibn Tulun travelled to the Syrian city to await al-Mu'tamid and his entourage; the caliph, following correspondence with Ibn Tulun, sought to decamp to Egypt. The effort collapsed with the caliph's arrest and his unceremonious return to Samarra, all engineered by al-Muwaffaq. Ibn Tulun, in response, organized a gathering of schol-ars, jurists and notables (Ar., *ashrāf*), calling on them to support his defense of al-Mu'tamid and censure of al-Muwaffaq. The latter's con-duct, Ibn Tulun insisted, violated the sanctity of the caliphate. It was thus only proper that he be removed as heir apparent, to which Ibn Tulun added a declaration of *jihad* against the regent.

As Luke Treadwell has suggested, the governor may well have been deeply troubled, on religious and ethical grounds, by al-Muwaffaq's treatment of his brother and, by extension, the caliphate. But we need also to consider the extent of Ibn Tulun's ambitions. There was, first of all, the setting. Ibn Tulun likely staged the event in the principal mosque of Damascus, a splendid early eighth-century Umayyad struc-ture. (The governor might have preferred to stage the assembly in his own mosque in al-Qata'i`, but circumstances dictated otherwise.) The venue was not only public but, in ideological terms, the most logical choice, as it placed Ibn Tulun in a highly visible religious setting. That he intended the assembly to be as public as possible is evinced by the choice of setting, but also Ibn Tulun's decision to have copies of the censure document read aloud in the principal mosques of the prov-inces under his authority.

The assembly was an audacious step. But, if the events in question seem clear enough – al-Kindi and al-Balawi provide detailed accounts – an explanation of Ibn Tulun's motivations is less so. He sought cen-ter stage, but with what specific outcome in mind? One recalls that Ibn Tulun faced a deteriorating situation in Tarsus, the confrontation with al-Muwaffaq, and the fallout from Lu'lu''s defection. These complications were compounded by the apparent conspiracy to have al-Mu'tamid transfer to Egypt. It is reasonable to suppose that Ibn Tulun hoped to mitigate, with a bold gesture, the various crises at once and, in this fashion, seal the argument over his political standing.

It was not to be. Of the questions raised by the Damascus Assembly, one concerns Bakkar ibn Qutayba and Ibn Tulun's relations with Sunni religious circles. Again, in Damascus, backed by two of his Egyptian colleagues, Bakkar offered only guarded support of Ibn Tulun's platform. Ibn Tulun responded by ordering Bakkar's arrest and public humiliation. One later Egyptian source has the elderly judge, badly clad, led through al-Fustat atop a pack animal. We are left to imagine how the event appeared to local onlookers; there are many indications that Bakkar was held in high regard in Egypt. Various sources speak of his tomb as having become the site of visitation (like that of al-Shafi'i). Bakkar himself responded when Ibn Tulun sought later to repair what had been, prior to the confrontation, a working relationship. The governor, for example, offered to pay off Bakkar's debts. Approached by Nasim, Ibn Tulun's envoy, Bakkar not only rejected the offer, but insisted on remaining in his cell, a clear show of defiance.

It seems fair to connect the confrontation to growing religio-legal divisions in Egypt. Bakkar was a leading light of the Hanafi school, yet another of the proto-Sunni circles in Egypt. It cannot be ruled out that Ibn Tulun's decision to punish Bakkar was calculated in part to appeal to his Shafi'i supporters. Ibn Tulun, in any case, walked a narrow line, in which, like other secular leaders of the age, he had to balance an assertion of authority with at least a public show of support for elite religious sentiments. The effort to exploit religion for political gain was by no means assured of success: if Ibn Tulun felt it necessary to punish Bakkar, he likely did so at no small cost to his public standing.

A further question concerns Ibn Tulun's relations with the Abbasid court. The confrontation with al-Muwaffaq turned initially on Ibn Tulun's refusal to accede to his rival's demands for revenue. The governor held his ground, but ultimately and despite Ibn Tulun's dramatic rebuke of the Abbasid regent in Damascus, the latter retained the stronger hand. This is evident not only in his alliance with Lu'lu' but in his ability to frustrate the apparent plan to relocate the caliphal court to Egypt. Ibn Tulun, it is true, had been able to demonstrate his backing for the caliph and the sanctity of his office; in this sense, he likely scored ideological points. But, on balance, it seems, Ibn Tulun departed Damascus with the value of his political stock much reduced relative to that of his rival.

Why did Ibn Tulun attempt a high-stakes gamble of this sort (the relocation of the caliphate from Iraq)? The biographies frame the question in terms of the governor's righteous views. Rejecting sound advice – that the governor would be overshadowed politically by the sovereign presence in al-Fustat – Ibn Tulun, having taken the oath to defend the caliph, pressed ahead on (pious) principle. An alternative explanation, however, goes to relations with the Abbasid court as a legitimating source. Ibn Tulun, again, never sought a break with the Abbasid center in the sense of asserting independence. A better reading is that he sought a rebalance of imperial authority; the presence of the Abbasid ruler and his court on the banks of the Nile would have served this purpose nicely. Ibn Tulun may well have conceived of it as a potential cornerstone of his new politics. But, again, the sources offer no clear explanation of Ibn Tulun's intentions: was the relocation scheme a well-laid plan or an act of improvisation? It is difficult to say.

The indications, in any case, are that Ibn Tulun overplayed his hand. On military and fiscal grounds, he laid the foundation for a strong dynastic polity. In this manner he demonstrated his political and administrative abilities. But he chose to press on by laying claim to Syria and the frontier districts and, on ideological grounds, framing a bold political agenda. A clear understanding of his thinking lies beyond our reach, but the impression is that Ibn Tulun, for all of his ambition, ventured too deeply into uncharted waters. This is evident also from the accounts of his two appearances on the frontier.

A brief recap. Al-Mu'tamid appointed Ibn Tulun over the frontier districts around 875–876, despite al-Muwaffaq's opposition. Only two years later – the delay is left unexplained – Ibn Tulun proceeded north into Syria and on to Tarsus, where he settled sometime in 878–880. There he faced resistance from the local populace, angry over the presence of the Tulunid forces and its impact on the local economy.

He responded by withdrawing from the city without a fight. Al-Balawi has Ibn Tulun's commanders argue the decision, in response to which Ibn Tulun used the excuse that an apparent capitulation would serve to fool the Byzantines into thinking that Tarsus was no easy target (if and when they decided to attack the city). He departed the frontier, in sum, without having secured a lasting presence and, thus, access to its ideological manna.

Lu'lu''s decision in 882 precipitated the governor's second march to Tarsus. Learning of his client's betrayal – and the political and military benefits that accrued to al-Muwaffaq – Ibn Tulun departed Egypt, and, following the events in Damascus, made for the frontier. On reaching Tarsus, this in the winter of 883, Ibn Tulun confronted new resistance from the city's inhabitants, now allied with Yazman, a client, possibly, of al-Muwaffaq. It is to be recalled that Yazman, drawing on local support, had ousted Ibn Tulun's resident governor the previous year. Ibn Tulun ordered a siege laid on Tarsus – proof enough, it would seem, that his standing on the frontier had deteriorated – but was soon forced to withdraw following the deliberate flooding of his camp.

Ibn Tulun had first traveled to the frontier as a young volunteer, eager, one is told, to take up the cause of *jihad*. Al-Balawi would have the governor retain a deep attachment to frontier and *jihad* alike. One notes a parallel with the commitment to *jihad* of the part of the Aghlabids in the central Mediterranean. In this sense, as well, Ibn Tulun can be thought of as a keen student of contemporary politics. But al-Balawi, in subtle fashion and, again, wielding the device of the anecdote, offers a pointed reminder of the change in Ibn Tulun's standing. In one story, for example, he has Ibn Tulun, during the first of his two appearances in Tarsus, meet with a local sage. The latter, described as a papyrus merchant turned frontier ascetic, admonishes Ibn Tulun for succumbing to the lure of politics and its trappings. Ibn Tulun erupts in tears.

It is a reminder of Ibn Tulun's pious turn. But it has a ring of truth, nonetheless, in suggesting that Ibn Tulun – now an imperial-style political broker – could no longer count on the embrace of his one-time frontier companions. A hallmark of ninth-century frontier culture was its resistance to imperial authority; relations between the Abbasid state and the religious leadership in Tarsus grew badly strained, a dynamic to which al-Balawi's anecdote likely refers. It seems altogether plausible, in other words, that Ibn Tulun and his foreign troops would have met with such a reception. It constituted but one step in the downturn of Ibn Tulun's fortunes. Each of the two occasions, like the falling out with Bakkar and the collapse of al-Mu`tamid's conspiracy, was a setback on both political and ideological grounds. Ibn Tulun, humiliated and seriously ill, had little option but to return to Egypt.

The care with which Ibn Tulun prepared for the succession of Khumarawayh makes sense in this context. Rebuffed in Syria and embarrassed on the frontier, Ibn Tulun sought to reaffirm his authority. The public setting; the presence of his commanders, civilian supporters, and clients; and the reminder, uttered in person by the dying *amir*, of the obligations of loyalty, discipline, and piety: all bespeak Ibn Tulun's determination to transfer office in proper fashion. The ceremony was the last of Ibn Tulun's public gestures. Its success doubtlessly impressed many contemporaries; Abu al-Jaysh assumed office with a minimum of fuss. Near Eastern history is strewn with examples of succession arrangements gone awry. But not in this case. It was an achievement, all the more so if one considers the political setbacks endured by Ibn Tulun in his final years in office.

CONCLUSION:
TULUNID FORTUNES

Abu al-Jaysh Khumarawayh assumed office in 884. He inherited a
seasoned military, a thriving economy, and a coterie of experienced
household clients, commanders, and officials. Ibn Tulun had turned to
Abu al-Jaysh following al-Abbas's botched rebellion in 878. The handover placed Egypt under dynastic rule for the first time in the Islamic
period. It went smoothly but without formal acknowledgment by the
Abbasid state. In this sense, as in others, Ibn Tulun sought to redefine
center-province relations, with obvious impact on political conditions
across the empire.

But Ibn Tulun also bequeathed to his son a fistful of problems: the
confrontation with the Abbasid center; diminished authority over the
frontier districts; and a tenuous position in Syria. Unable to resolve
them, Abu al-Jaysh, like his father, would thus juggle success and
humiliation. He would govern for twelve years, falling to assassins –
members of his personal household – in 896. Things declined steadily
thereafter. In 905, Abbasid units under Muhammad ibn Sulayman
seized al-Qata'i`. Ibn Sulayman saw to the destruction of much of the
Tulunid capital, the exile (to Baghdad) of the surviving members of
the Tulunid family, and the crushing of resistance by Tulunid loyalist
forces. A thirty-year period of imperial rule over Egypt followed.

The Tulunid state – Ibn Tulun's experiment – collapsed for many
reasons. The most immediate cause were developments in Syria. Shi`i
opponents to Abbasid rule had remained active in southern Iraq into
the late ninth century. One such movement, the Qarmatis, rose in

Kufa and, over several decades, staged attacks against the caliphate in Iraq and Syria. In 902, Qarmati forces defeated Tulunid units and, following the defeat, a number of Tulunid officers, including Tughj ibn Juff, deserted to the Abbasids. The caliph, al-Muktafi (r. 902–908), seized the moment. He sent Muhammad ibn Sulayman against the Qarmatis and, following a victory over the rebels, Ibn Sulayman pressed on into Egypt. The Abbasid assault on al-Qata'i' followed.

Other factors included a crisis of Tulunid leadership: the last rulers of the dynasty were minors with none of the standing of Ibn Tulun and his son. Exacerbating the crisis were deep rivalries within the Tulunid family, officer corps and elite civilian circles. These were long-standing: Ibn Tulun, for all of his political savvy, good fortune, and fiscal resources, had failed to win over elite loyalties in lasting fashion. One can cite the examples of al-Abbas and Lu'lu'. Khumarawayh, early in his tenure, faced a similar shock: Ahmad al-Wasiti, long a mainstay of the Tulunid house, threw his support to al-Muwaffaq. Tulunid control over Egypt's fiscal resources and territory remained intact. But the integrity of the Tulunid household, maintained uneasily by Ibn Tulun and Khumarawayh, remained in question.

And there were new pressures on the Tulunid treasury. Khumarawayh spent much of the wealth that he had inherited from his father. This left the later Tulunids badly hobbled on fiscal as well as political grounds. If the many stories of Khumarawayh's excesses are contrived, they still leave the strong impression that he failed to learn the lessons of his father's fiscal discipline. He is reported to have spent lavishly, converting, for example, the famous Maydan into elaborate gardens that featured, among other eccentric touches, life-size statues of his favorite courtesans. Khumarawayh is also remembered for the sumptuous wedding in 892 of his daughter, Qatr al-Nada, to the sitting caliph, al-Mu'tadid (r. 892–902), at a cost of one million dinars. The Tulunid treasury might well have absorbed these costs: there is little reason to think that normal administration in Egypt was disrupted. Revenue continued to flow. But the new expenditures came on top of new levels of military spending in particular. Khumarawayh, like his father, spent much time on campaign, mostly in Syria and, at home in Egypt, turned to his forces on a regular basis.

Further political and fiscal ills emerged from Khumarawayh's relations with the Abbasid center. Al-Muwaffaq kept up pressure following Ibn Tulun's death by supporting anti-Tulunid efforts in Syria. Khumarawayh, in response, opted for two agreements with the caliphate, the first in 886. Accounts of the agreement are brief and say little directly about fiscal arrangements. It provided the Tulunids with the right to govern Egypt and the Syrian provinces for a period of thirty years. Khumarawayh, having just returned from a campaign in Syria, ordered in response an end to the public cursing of al-Muwaffaq and formal recognition of Abbasid authority.

The agreement held for six years to the death of al-Muwaffaq in 892. A brief power struggle in Baghdad brought al-Muʿtadid to the throne. A strongman, the new monarch enjoyed close ties to the Samarran military. He adopted a two-fold policy toward the Tulunids. On the one hand, he acknowledged Tulunid authority in Egypt and Syria but, on the other, asserted Abbasid authority over much of the Jazira and the frontier districts, thus directly challenging Tulunid claims to these areas. This occurred in the context of a second Abbasid-Tulunid agreement (892), in which Tulunid authority was recognized again for a thirty-year period. Khumarawayh, in exchange, agreed to a substantial annual tribute and handover of areas of the Jazira. The marriage of Qatr al-Nada to al-Muʿtadid occurred at just this point.

The new arrangements are not easily interpreted. Khumarawayh, like his father, continued work to legitimate the Tulunid house. The marriage furthered this aim in providing for closer ties to the imperial house. More difficult to understand is the thirty-year agreement. As a new caliph, seeking to consolidate authority, al-Muʿtadid may have been seeking breathing space. But what of the stipulation regarding the payment of tribute? It seems that no such agreement existed under Ibn Tulun: the evidence is that the founder of the Tulunid state never submitted *regular* payments to Abbasid Iraq. One reading is that the agreement was an effort to exact new pressures on the Tulunid state.

Khumarawayh's assassination in Damascus followed in 896. It is telling that he died in Syria, in pursuit of the territories first taken by his father. The latter's ambition of bringing together the frontier districts, Syria, the Jazira, Egypt, and probably the Hijaz thus remained unfulfilled. In the attempt to achieve this one goal alone, Abu al-Jaysh, like his father, overreached and, in his case, with diminished fiscal resources in hand. But, by the same token, it is a measure of all that Ibn Tulun had achieved in Egypt that Khumarawayh could pursue matters as vigorously as he did. In Egypt, the Tulunid house retained considerable support. Al-Balawi, in his account of the succession ceremony for Abu al-Jaysh, has the *amir* acknowledge to his heir that it – the Tulunid polity – was as a "thorn in the side of the caliphate." To extract it, the Abbasids had little recourse but outright military assault.

THE *AMIR*'S CAREER

There remains more to say of Ibn Tulun's tenure in office, particularly in relation to Abbasid imperial history. The Arab-Islamic Empire emerged under Abbasid rule as a wealthy, cosmopolitan, and deeply Islamic polity with the caliphate tapping creatively into long-established Near Eastern monarchical traditions. The Abbasids, drawing on Byzantine and Sasanid patterns, created a new model of imperial authority. The model succeeded, but only for a time. The early Abbasids sustained a sprawling, bureaucratic state, bound by the appeal to religion, the wealth of Iraq and Egypt, and the authority of the Iraqi center. The humiliations of the ninth century followed, however, with the empire eventually giving way to a regional system – including Egypt – that took shape from the tenth century on.

Two elements endured: the idea of an Islamic political unity and the authority that attached to the caliphate. If that same authority turned mostly symbolic from the early tenth century on, the process was gradual. One needs no better indication than the fact that, even in the late ninth century, lessened as it was, the Abbasid house could still engineer the destruction of the Tulunid house.

This is to see the Tulunid "moment" as a point of transition. The setbacks of the ninth century, especially in Iraq, did indeed reduce imperial fortunes. The costs were, in part, ideological. The execution of a seated caliph – al-Amin in 813 – had been one turning point, and others followed. If the office of caliph remained sacrosanct, as it did, the standing of individual caliphs was much diminished. The aggressions of the military command in Samarra demonstrated as much. So, too, al-Muwaffaq's intervention in imperial decision-making. Ibn Tulun, a son of Samarra, took this lesson on board. Abbasid authority could be negotiated.

Setbacks for the empire were also fiscal. Egyptian revenue, second in scale only to that of Iraq, were critical to the empire's future. In this sense, al-Muwaffaq, in his demands on Ibn Tulun, was voicing a wider anxiety fed by Ibn Tulun's achievements. The *amir* secured order over the Egyptian hinterlands, strengthened local administration, and dictated the pace of tribute payments to the empire. In such manner, Ibn Tulun made clear the level of wealth that Egypt was capable of producing, and the manner in which control of that same wealth could be achieved.

It is in this sense that Ibn Tulun's project was transitional. To repeat a point made earlier, Ibn Tulun can be seen to have acted prematurely: he left his heir a political puzzle that was near impossible to solve. Tulunid ambitions might have flourished in some later context but, at this point, the imperial house still had on hand sufficient resources to push back. That said, Ibn Tulun's effort was not only impressive in its scope but also offered a working model for future political claimants. Following Ibn Sulayman's assault in 905, the Abbasid center secured formal authority in Egypt for some thirty years. But it was an unsettled period: Abbasid authority in the Nile Valley reached its practical limits. Efforts to sustain (Tulunid-style) fiscal policies sparked rounds of rural unrest, while, in al-Fustat itself, factional infighting badly divided the local military and its command. Conditions in Egypt came to resemble those of Syria.

The violence came to an uneasy close with the ascent of Muhammad ibn Tughj ibn Juff. His father, a one-time Tulunid commander, had switched earlier to the Abbasid side. In governing Egypt, Ibn Tughj adopted the title of *ikhshid*, a traditional Central Asian honorific. Ibn Tughj's tenure (935–946) resembled that of Ahmad ibn Tulun: he exploited Egyptian revenue to consolidate authority and struggled – using a mix of negotiation and force – to impose order in Syria. There, resistance to Ikhshidid inroads came from the Abbasids but also the

Hamdanids, an Arab power in northern Syria. The Ikhshidid period, briefer than that of the Tulunids, closed with the regency of Kafur al-Labi (d. 968), a freedman of Nubian origin.

By this point, Abbasid authority was on the ropes. If the imperial center had once been able to frustrate the Tulunids, now it could only watch as Egypt slipped away. The Ikhshidids, and Kafur in particular, faced not only opposition in Syria but a significant threat from the Fatimid state. The Fatimids, an Isma`ili Shi`i movement, had established themselves in Ifriqiya in the early tenth century. Drawing on local support, the Fatimids proclaimed a new caliphate in 909 in direct challenge to the Abbasids. Fatimid designs on Egypt emerged quickly, with three campaigns in 915, 920, and 935. Following a decades-long respite, Fatimid troops finally overran al-Fustat in 969. The new dynasty would govern from al-Qahira (Cairo), its new capital, for some two hundred years (969–1171). In contrast with Ibn Tulun's ambiguous effort to redefine ties to the Abbasid center, the Fatimid stance was clear: the new dynasty declared its opposition to, indeed its intent to destroy, the Abbasid state.

Ibn Tulun's career thus spanned a short but compelling period of Egypt's history. This book has sought to make two points. The first is that a careful study that combines a reading of the written, documentary, and material sources allows for a reconstruction of Ibn Tulun's tenure in office. The second point is that the written sources devote considerable space to representing his career. The key texts are the biographies of Ibn al-Daya and al-Balawi, the latter the more detailed and thus more significant source. How do they weigh Ibn Tulun's career? It is worth reading a further anecdote from al-Balawi's *Sira*. It has Ibn Tulun react to a perceived political slight but, seeing the matter resolved, not only relent but extend a generous hand.

> Siwar *al-khadim* [a palace official] recounted the following: "Ibn Tulun attended the Friday prayer. The preacher, atop the *minbar* [typically a tall structure at the front of the mosque, from which the prayer leader (Ar., *imam*) conducts the khutba and leads worship], ended the sermon with the names of al-Mu`tamid and his sons, but neglected to mention Ahmad ibn Tulun. As he stepped down the *minbar*, Ibn Tulun motioned to me and said: 'If he completes the prayer session and exits the mosque,

have him lashed five hundred times.' The *imam*, his foot on the last step, realized his error, scrambled back up the *minbar* and said: 'Praise God and His blessings on Muhammad. *For We had made a covenant before with Adam but he forgot, and We found no firm resolve on his part.* God, in Your glory, see to the *amir*, Ahmad ibn Tulun!' He added further words of commendation then stepped down. My master ordered me to compensate him well. The preacher, informed of Ibn Tulun's response, praised the Almighty for His protection. Those in attendance rushed to him with words of congratulation and relief."

The story, like the earlier anecdote about Umm Uqba, sets Ibn Tulun in a real-life setting (and with a similar humorous twist). The Friday communal prayer, a long-established element of Arab-Islamic political culture, offered leaders a public moment. It turned on the acknowledgment of authority: the preacher's task was to attach an appeal for divine guidance to the names of the appropriate office holders, that is, the caliph, his heirs, *and* the governor. It was a declaration of submission and loyalty. To neglect a name from the list was to issue a political challenge.

Whether or not the episode occurred does not matter. These stories frequently worked as commentary, in some cases light-hearted, in other cases more serious. In the case of al-Balawi's *Sira*, many such stories fall closer to the sober end of the spectrum. They ask readers to take the measure of Ibn Tulun's leadership. At issue, especially, was the question of justice: in what measure was he driven by piety, mercy, sound advice, and the transparent use of public wealth?

Al-Balawi, like Ibn al-Daya, saw Ibn Tulun as an appropriate foil. This is to argue, in other words, that the *amir* served as an appropriate model for consideration. The many stories provided by both authors work – or, at least, presumably, worked for the medieval authors and their readers – precisely because of the *amir*'s calculated approach to office. Behind the stories lay a political drama that unfolded in real time. This is to see Ibn Tulun as a close student of politics and a determined office holder.

At issue throughout was his bid for a new-style form of authority. To succeed, he had to overcome a deficit of political capital. He faced, first of all, questions regarding his background and commitment to the Islamic tradition. His biographers provide ready answers. They describe the process by which Ibn Tulun overcame his origins. He was, after all, a "Turk," with all the uneasy association that attached to that tag for an early medieval Near Eastern reader. He did so by dint of service to the caliphate, seriousness of purpose, and proper religious (read: Islamic) training. He honed these qualities on the Byzantine-Islamic frontier and his long sojourn with ascetic warriors and scholars. These passages are to be read alongside a number of other Abbasid-era texts that reflect the low opinion with which many contemporaries viewed the Samarran soldiers. They were, the view seems to be, outsiders with little appreciation of Islam. Such barely concealed disdain likely reflected long-standing views of sedentary folk toward nomadic or frontier – thus, in this view, only partly civilized – peoples, the Other of Near Eastern urban society.

These public issues may have lain dormant had it not been for the emergence of the Turkic-Central Asian military. The Samarran soldiers challenged the authority of the caliphate, in making and breaking Abbasid office holders, and in laying claim to significant fiscal and military resources, notably the wealth of Egypt. Boundaries were crossed: these claims, for most observers, were unacceptable. It is likely that such attitudes followed Ibn Tulun to Egypt. His initial appointment was that of resident governor, with defined duties to serve the empire as his predecessors had before him. To many inhabitants of Egypt, this was sufficient reason for opposition: he represented Abbasid authority in a province with a long history of resisting imperial fiscal and political demands. That he was of "alien" origin only fueled the argument.

Questions arose from the start but became all the more pressing as his political ambitions grew. Had he indeed overcome his origins with a proper embrace of Islam? How meaningful was that embrace? How would he negotiate his relations with the Abbasid center, on the one hand, the Samarran military command, on the other? How would he serve the people of Egypt? The indications are that Ibn Tulun acted creatively and with great energy.

But on what basis did he proceed? The question has several parts. There is the matter of Ibn Tulun's selection as governor. It remains unclear as to why Bayakbak, followed by Yarjukh – in consultation, one supposes, with the caliphal administration – saw Ibn Tulun as a likely candidate. As noted earlier, there is almost no evidence of prior administrative or command experience on Ibn Tulun's part. Rather, the biographers would have us believe that Bayakbak's circle of officers and civilian allies, caught up as they were in Samarra's turmoil, valued Ibn Tulun's moral qualities over his ability to govern. The sources, in sum, seem content with the explanation that Ibn Tulun had impressed his superiors with the strength of his character and, on that basis, they dispatched him to Egypt.

These same questions have also to do with the resources – human, material, and ideological – at Ibn Tulun's disposal. We have to think that Ibn Tulun carefully weighed his position once in office in al-Fustat. He had done well, initially in Tarsus, then later in Iraq. If he was to succeed in Egypt, however, he would have to cultivate resources locally. And there remains that most interesting question: when did he think it possible to make a bid for full authority over Egypt? If Ibn Tulun did not seek a sharp break with the empire – and this book argues that he did not – he pursued nonetheless a pattern of governance, long unfamiliar to the Nile Valley, that made it certainly possible. It was a project in which Ibn Tulun brought together established political, religious, and fiscal ingredients into a new repertoire of power. It was, in its way, a subtle approach. On at least two occasions, for example, Ibn Tulun was content to deliver revenue to Samarra. He also kept the name of the reigning caliph on all coinage minted on his initiative; left off outright military confrontation with his detractors in Iraq; and, throughout, retained his affiliation with at least the seated caliph, al-Mu'tamid.

This is some of the evidence that one can bring to the argument that Ibn Tulun never considered independence from the Abbasid caliphate. But why did he forgo that aim? There is much to indicate, after all, that Ibn Tulun had the means on hand with which to create a self-standing, dynastic state. The answer is that Ibn Tulun constructed something rather more complicated (and, thus, perhaps, more difficult to govern than an independent state). His aim was a redefinition of relations between the imperial çenter and the provinces or, put differently, a different model of empire-province relations. He achieved a delicate balance of homage to the authority of the Abbasid throne in exchange for allowance to pursue aims of his own. His suppression of local opposition in Egypt, to take one example of the *amir*'s efforts, allowed not simply for tighter control over Egypt and its considerable revenue but served also the needs of both the imperial house and the Sunni religious establishment.

And what of the longer-term effect of Ibn Tulun's experiment? This last question goes to how other regional polities of this and later periods viewed Ibn Tulun's tenure in office. Post-Tulunid Egypt fell to individuals and dynasties with obvious local ambitions, beginning with Muhammad ibn Tughj al-Ikhshid and Kafur al-Labi, and continuing on through the Fatimids and Ayyubids to the great Mamluk rulers of the later medieval period. Much the same can be said of Khurasan and other provinces of the once unitary Arab-Islamic realm. Again, by the mid-tenth century, the era of unitary Near Eastern politics had ended. Ibn Tulun's efforts were thus both a symptom of, and contributing factor to, imperial disintegration and the spread of regionalized politics.

There is reason to think that later power brokers looked to Ibn Tulun's example. His approach to office offered a template. If later dynasts chose to use its ingredients in different combinations, Ibn Tulun's recipe offered a compelling *style* of governance. What indications are there that his example was considered closely? We can point to the frequency with which Ibn Tulun and Khumarawayh appear in later biographical collections and other writings. It is striking that later Near Eastern chroniclers, compilers of biographical dictionaries, poets, and other writers – many of whom wrote in expectation of official support – comment at length on Ibn Tulun's career. It is in this sense, in his pursuit of principled governance, however roughly executed, that his example struck a chord.

ACKNOWLEDGMENTS

I would first thank Khaled El-Rouayheb and Sabine Schmidtke for agreeing to include this volume in the series, and the team at Oneworld – Jonathan Bentley-Smith, Paul Nash, Elizabeth Hinks – for their fine editorial and production work. A great number of friends, students, and colleagues contributed to the making of this book, and I am deeply grateful for their support, wisdom, and information. My hope is that this list is complete: Manan Ahmed, Jere Bacharach, Michael Bates, Sheila Blair, Jonathan Bloom, Michael Bonner, Antoine Borrut, Jelle Bruning, Michael Cook, Patricia Crone, Tayeb El-Hibri, Gladys Frantz-Murphy, Marie Legendre, Tamara Maatouk, Maged Mikhail, Alastair Northedge, Bilal Orfali, Hani Ramadan, Ernest Randa, Chase Robinson, Petra Sijpesteijn, Tarek Swelim, Mathieu Tillier, Luke Treadwell, and Naïm Vanthieghem. Jeremiah and Kate heard probably more about Ibn Tulun than they deserved, as did Susan, to whom, with such gratitude, I dedicate this book.

BIBLIOGRAPHY

Ibn Tulun has long been of interest to modern scholars. This book draws, alongside a number of Arabic sources, on secondary works on the governor's life and times. These include Zaky Mohamed Hassan's monograph (1933); Ernest Randa's unpublished doctoral dissertation (1990); and Thierry Bianquis's narrative essay on the Tulunid era (1998). Each work facilitates the task of recovering Ibn Tulun's career. I have also made use of more specialized studies of the Tulunid period, including the work of Gladys Frantz-Murphy on the early medieval Egyptian economy; Oleg Grabar's study of Tulunid numismatics; Michael Bonner's study of the Damascus Assembly of 269/883; Luke Treadwell's study of Tulunid coinage; and Mathieu Tillier's writings on the Abbasid-era judiciary and the Tulunid reign.

SUGGESTED READING

Bacharach, Jere, 1991. "Administrative Complexes, Palaces, and Citadels: Change in the Loci of Medieval Muslim Rule." In *The Ottoman City and Its Parts: Urban Structure and Social Order*, eds, Irene A. Bierman et al., New Rochelle, N.Y.: A.D. Caratzes: 111–128.

Bianquis, Thierry, 1998. "Autonomous Egypt from Ibn Tulun to Kafur, 868–969." In Carl F. Petry, ed., *The Cambridge History of Egypt, Volume I: Islamic Egypt, 640–1517*, Cambridge: Cambridge University Press, 86–119.

Bonner, Michael, 2010. "Ibn Tulun's Jihad: The Damascus Assembly of 269/883." *Journal of the American Oriental Society* (130:4): 573–605.

Brett, Michael, 2010. "Egypt." In *The New Cambridge History of Islam*, vol. I, *The Formation of the Islamic World, Sixth to Eleventh Centuries*, ed. Chase F. Robinson,

Cambridge: Cambridge University Press, 541–580.

Bruning, Jelle, 2018. *The Rise of a Capital: Al-Fusṭāṭ and its Hinterland, 18/639–132/750*. Leiden: Brill.

Darling, Linda, 2013. *A History of Social Justice and Political Power in the Middle East: The Circle of Justice from Mesopotamia to Globalization*. London & New York: Routledge.

Frantz-Murphy, Gladys, 1981. "A New Interpretation of the Economic History of Medieval Egypt: The Role of the Textile Industry, 254–567/868–1171." *Journal of the Economic and Social History of the Orient* (24:3): 274–297.

Gordon, Matthew S., 2001. *The Breaking of a Thousand Swords: A History of the Turkish Military of Samarra (A.H. 200–275/815–889 C.E.)*. Albany, N.Y.: SUNY Press.

———. 2015. "Aḥmad ibn Ṭūlūn and the Politics of Deference." In Behnam Sadeghi et al., eds, *Islamic Cultures, Islamic Contexts: Essays in Honor of Professor Patricia Crone*. Leiden: Brill Publishing, 229–256.

Grabar, Oleg, 1957. *The Coinage of the Tulunids*. New York: The American Numismatic Society.

Hassan, Zaky Mohamed, 1933. *Les Tulunides: Etude de l'Egypte Musulmane à la fin du IXe Siècle, 868–905*. Paris: Établissements Busson.

Hunt, L. A. "Stuccowork at the monastery of the Syrians in the Wadî Natrun: Iraqi – Egyptian Artistic Contact in the 'Abbasid Period." In David Richard Thomas, ed., *Christians at the Heart of Islamic Rule: Church Life and Scholarship in 'Abbasid Iraq* (Leiden & Boston: Brill, 2003): 93–127.

Kennedy, Hugh, 1998. "Egypt as a province in the Islamic caliphate, 641–868." In Carl F. Petry, ed., *The Cambridge History of Egypt, Volume I: Islamic Egypt, 640–1517*, Cambridge: Cambridge University Press, 62–85.

———. 2004. *The Prophet and the Age of the Caliphates*, 2nd edition. Harlow, UK: Pearson Education Limited.

Mikhail, Maged S.A., 2014. *From Byzantine to Islamic Egypt: Religion, Identity and Politics after the Arab Conquest*. London: I.B. Tauris.

Morimoto, Kosei, 1981. *The Fiscal Administration of Egypt in the Early Islamic Period*. Kyoto: Dohosha Publishing.

Northedge, Alastair, 2005. *The Historical Topography of Samarra*. London: The British School of Archaeology in Iraq.

Petry, Carl F., ed. 1998. *The Cambridge History of Egypt, Volume I: Islamic Egypt, 640–1517*. Cambridge: Cambridge University Press.

Power, Timothy, 2012. *The Red Sea from Byzantium to the Caliphate, AD 500–1000*. Cairo: The American University of Cairo Press.

Randa, Ernest William Jr, 1990. *The Tulunid Dynasty in Egypt: Loyalty and State Formation during the Dissolution of the 'Abbasid Caliphate*. Ph.D. thesis, The University of Utah.

Sijpesteijn, Petra M. 2013. *Shaping a Muslim State: The World of a Mid-Eighth-Century Egyptian Official.* Oxford: Oxford University Press.

Swelim, M. Tarek, 2015. *Ibn Tulun: His Lost City and Great Mosque.* Cairo & New York: The American University in Cairo Press.

Tillier, Mathieu, 2011. "The *Qadi*s of Fustat-Misr under the Tulunids and the Ikhshidids: The Judiciary and Egyptian Autonomy." *Journal of the American Oriental Society* (131:2): 207–222.

———. 2015. "L'étoile, la châine et le Jugement. Essai d'interprétation d'un élément de décor dans la mosquée d'Ibn Ṭūlūn." *Der Islam* (92:2): 332–366.

Treadwell, Luke, 2017. "The Numismatic Evidence for the Reign of Aḥmad ibn Ṭūlūn (254–270/868–883)." *Al-Usur al-Wusta* (25): 14–40.

INDEX

References to images are in *italics*.